My Big Easter Coloring Book

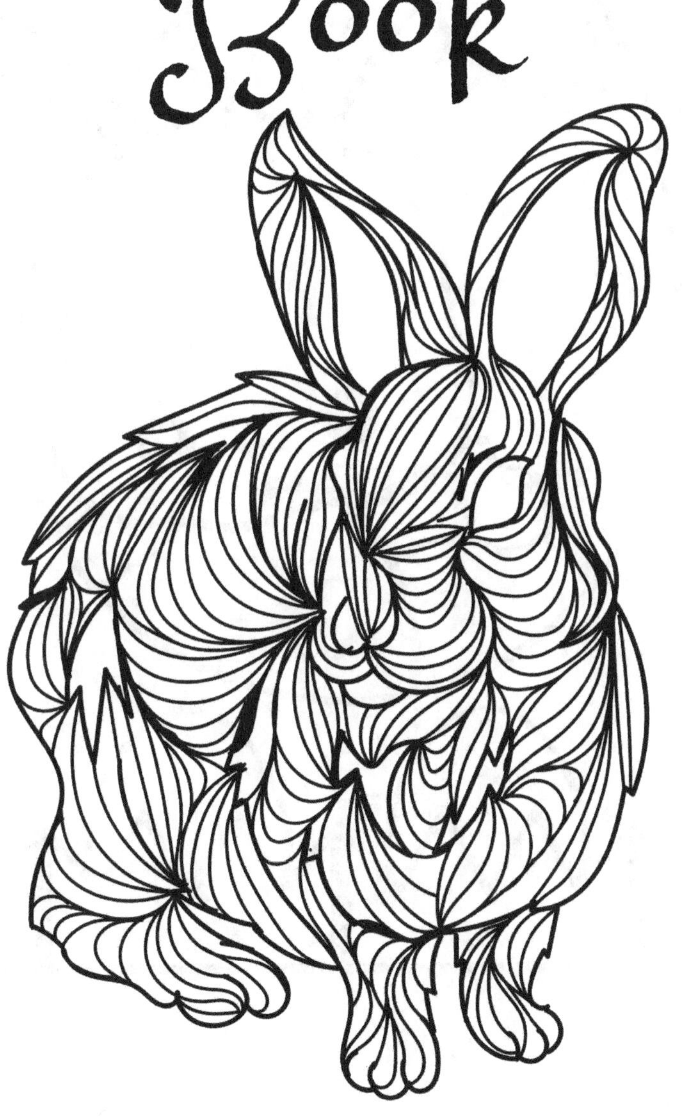

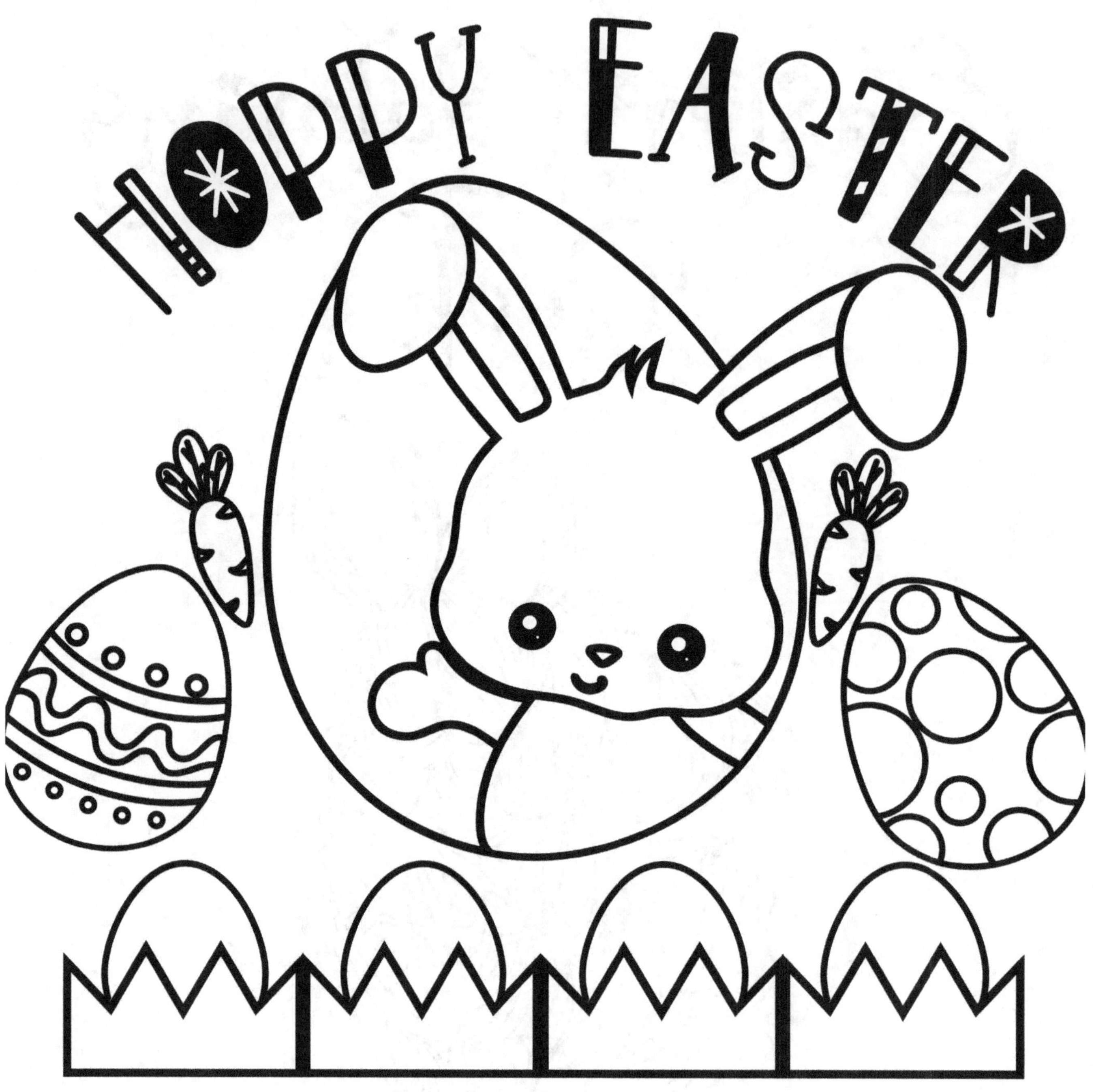
HOPPY EASTER

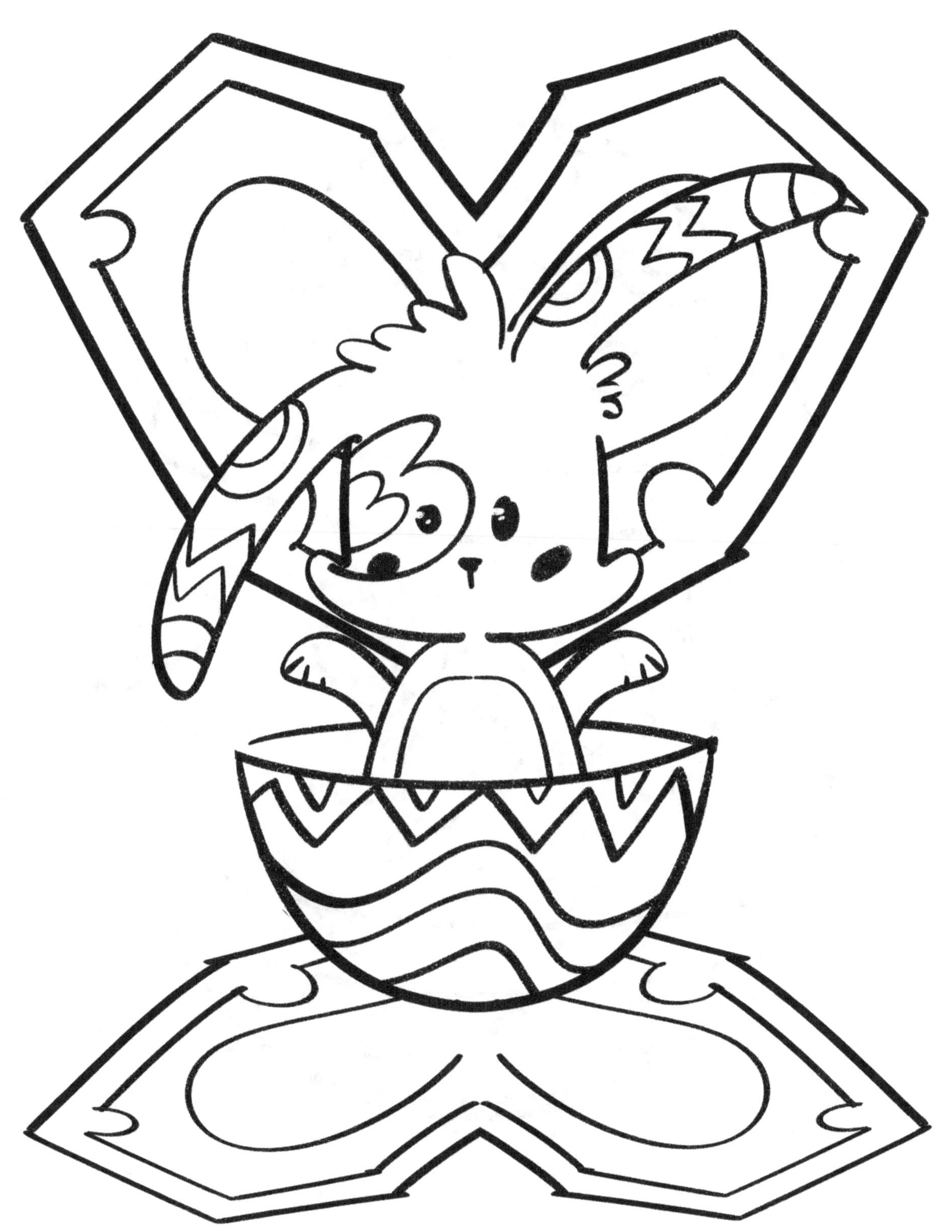

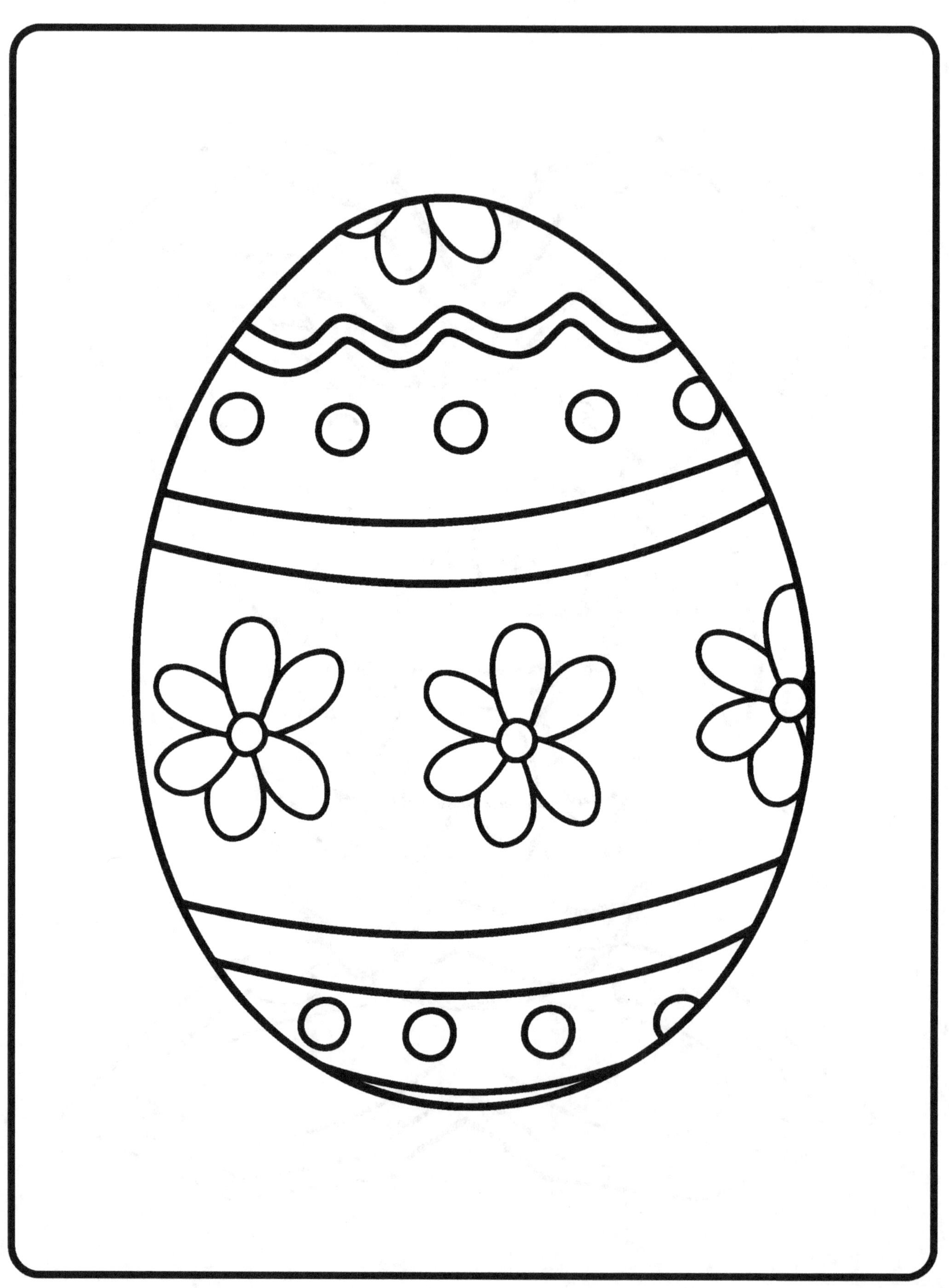

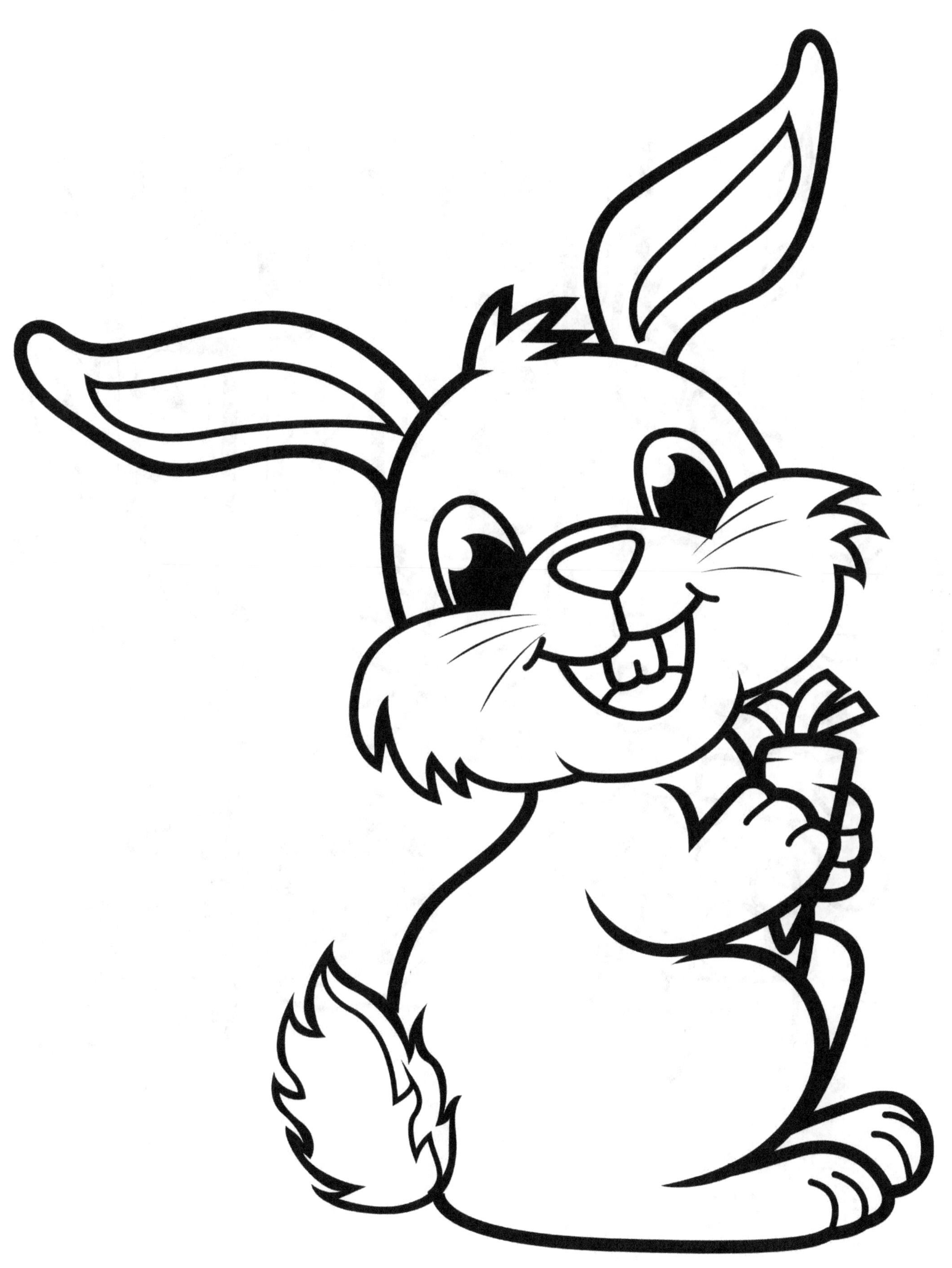

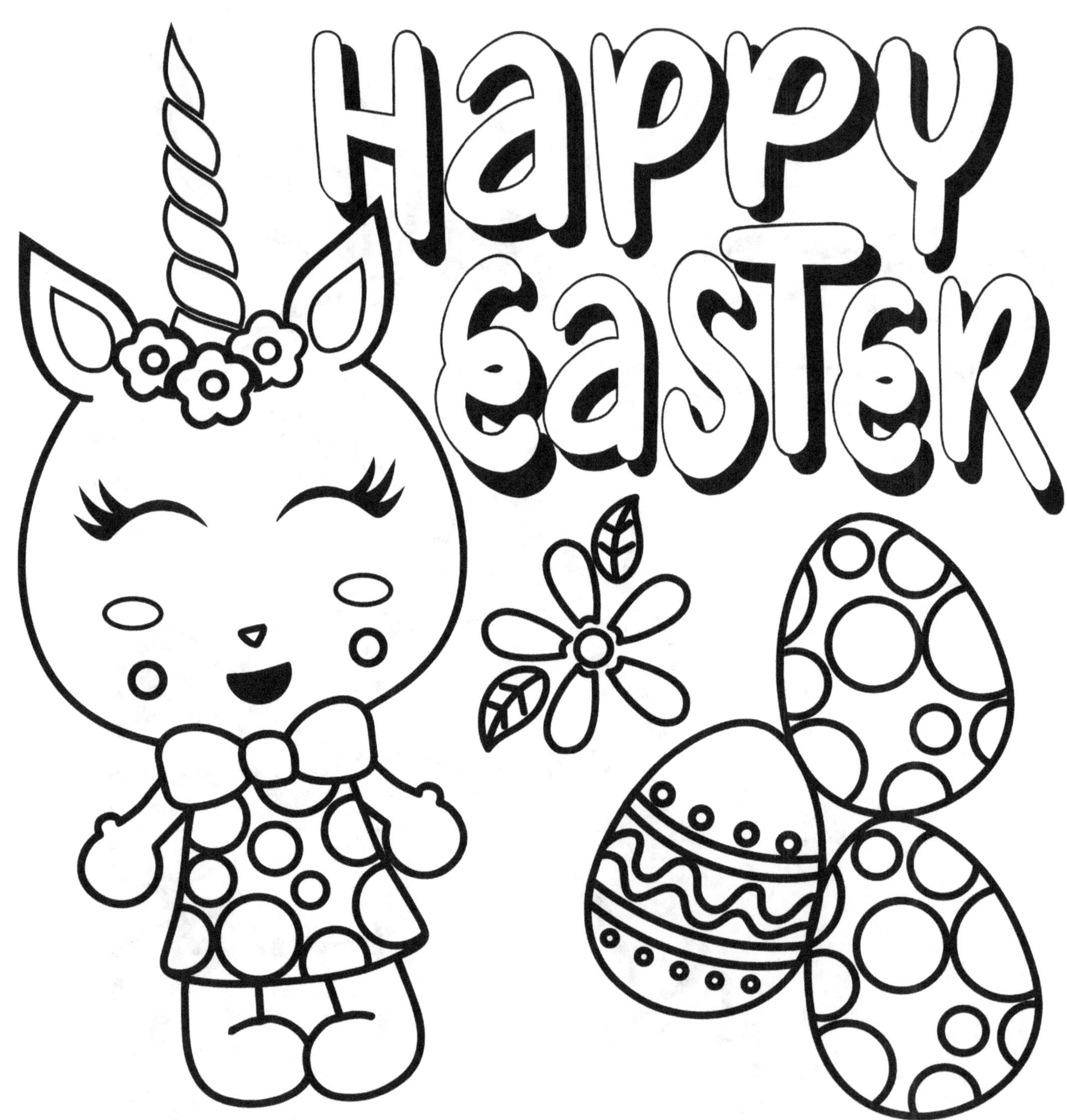

HAPPY
EASTER

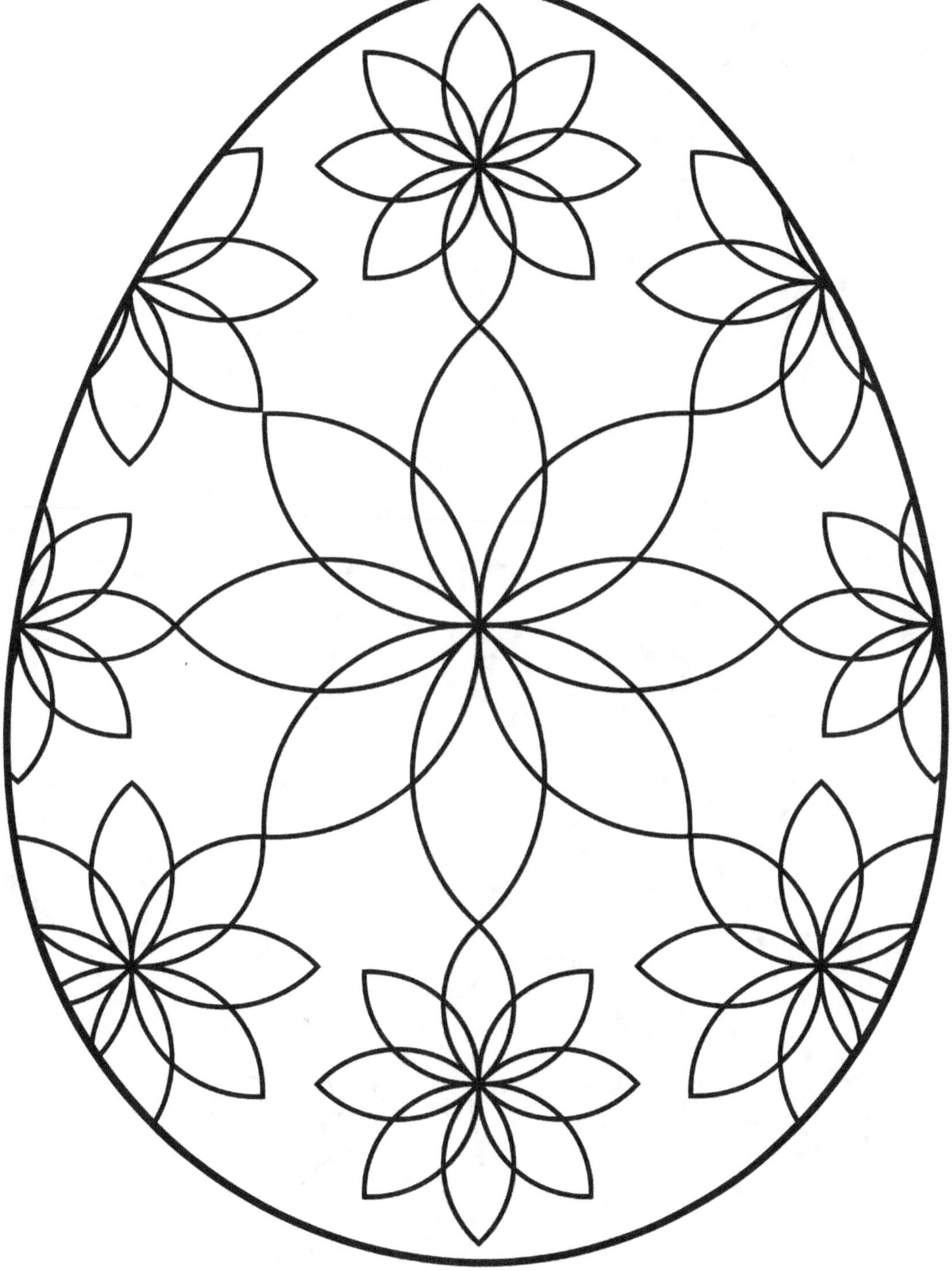

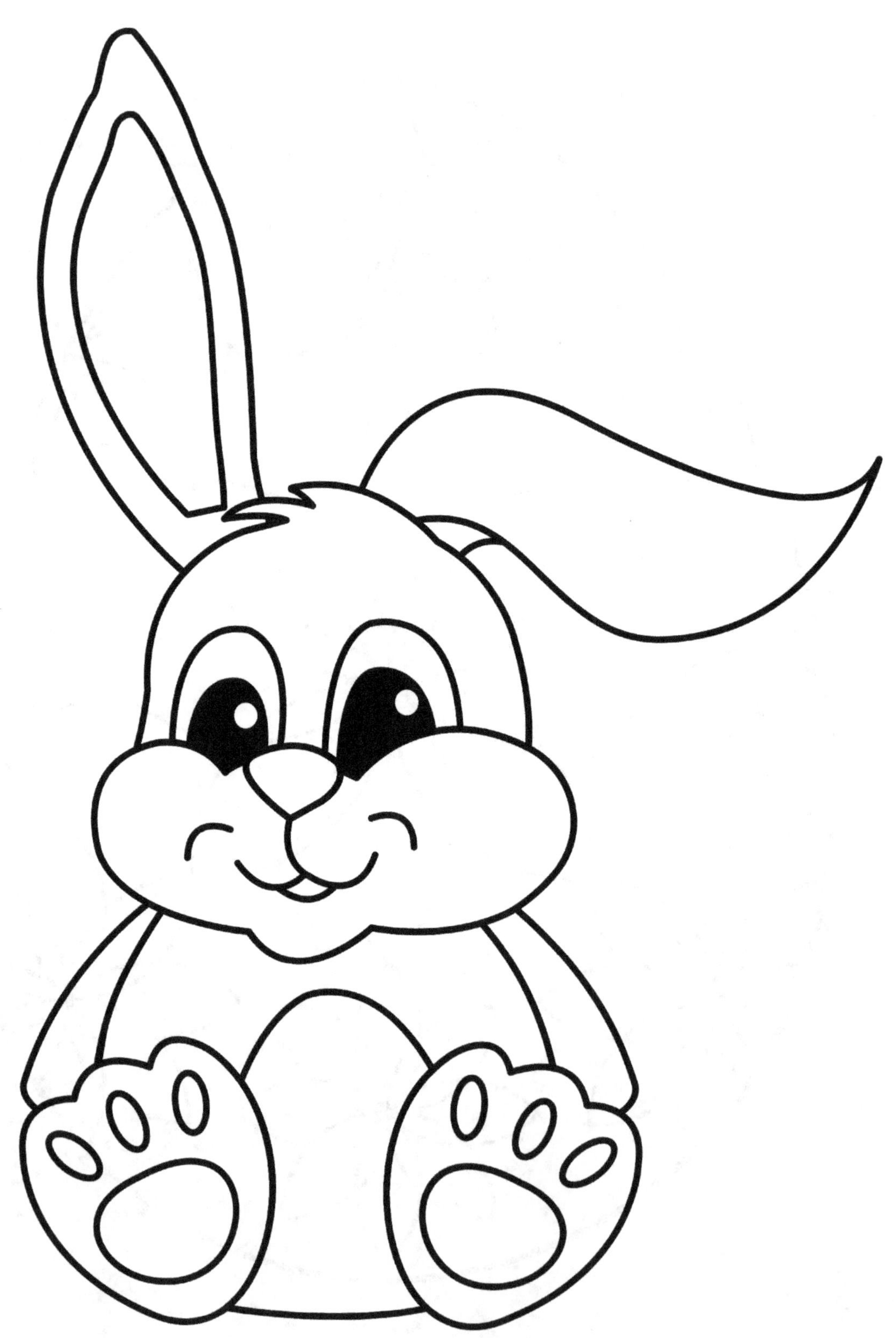

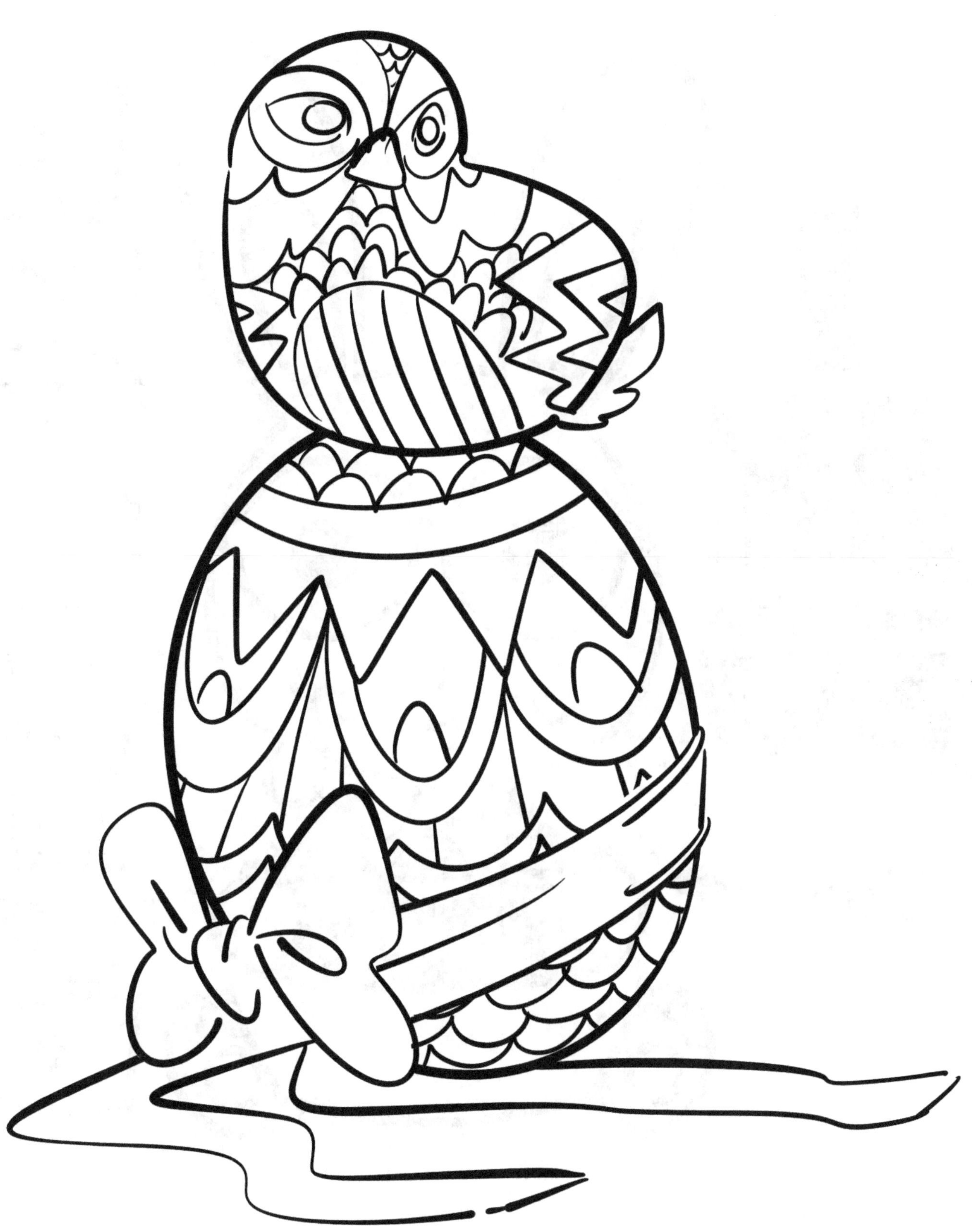

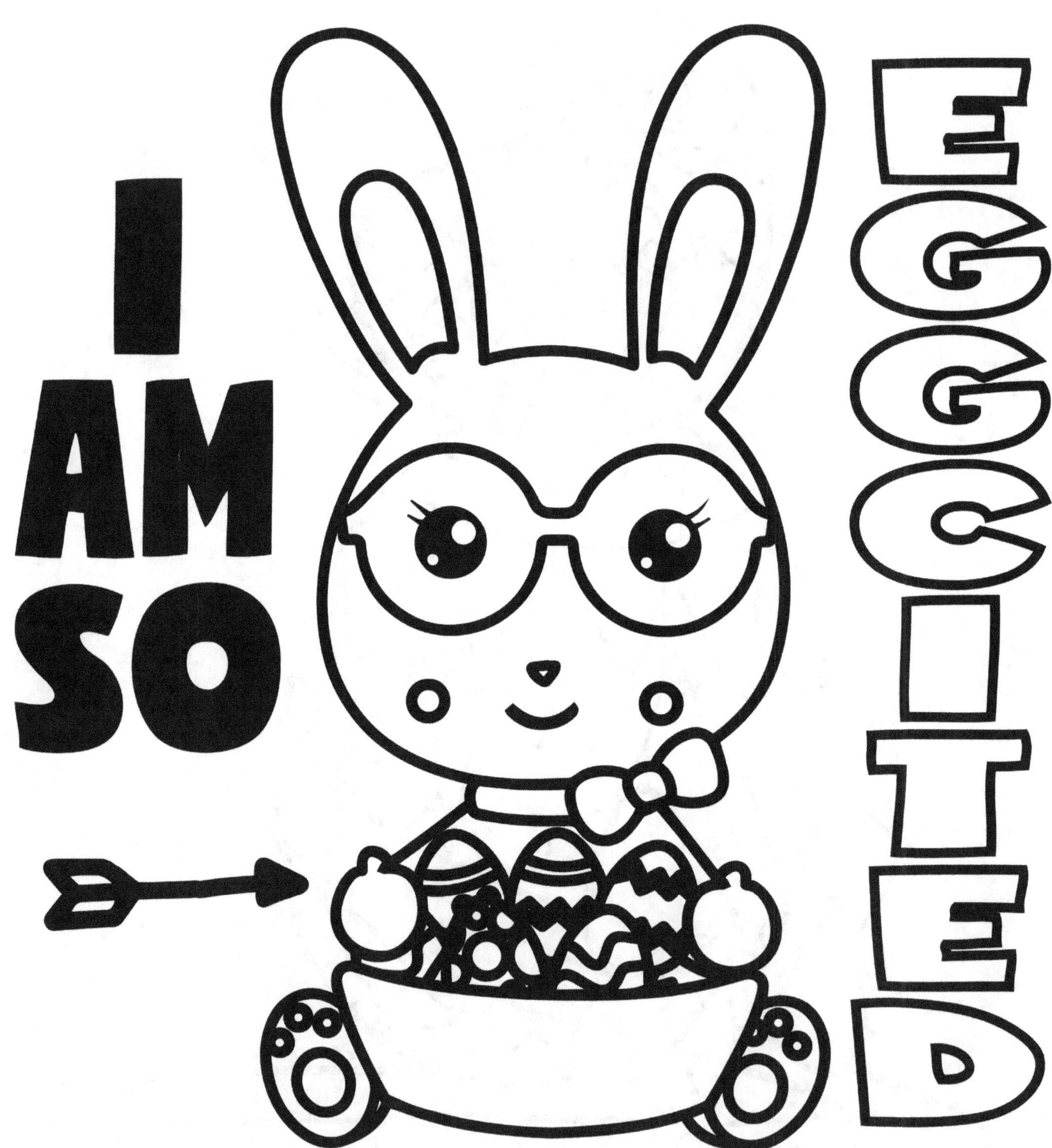

I AM SO
EGGCITED

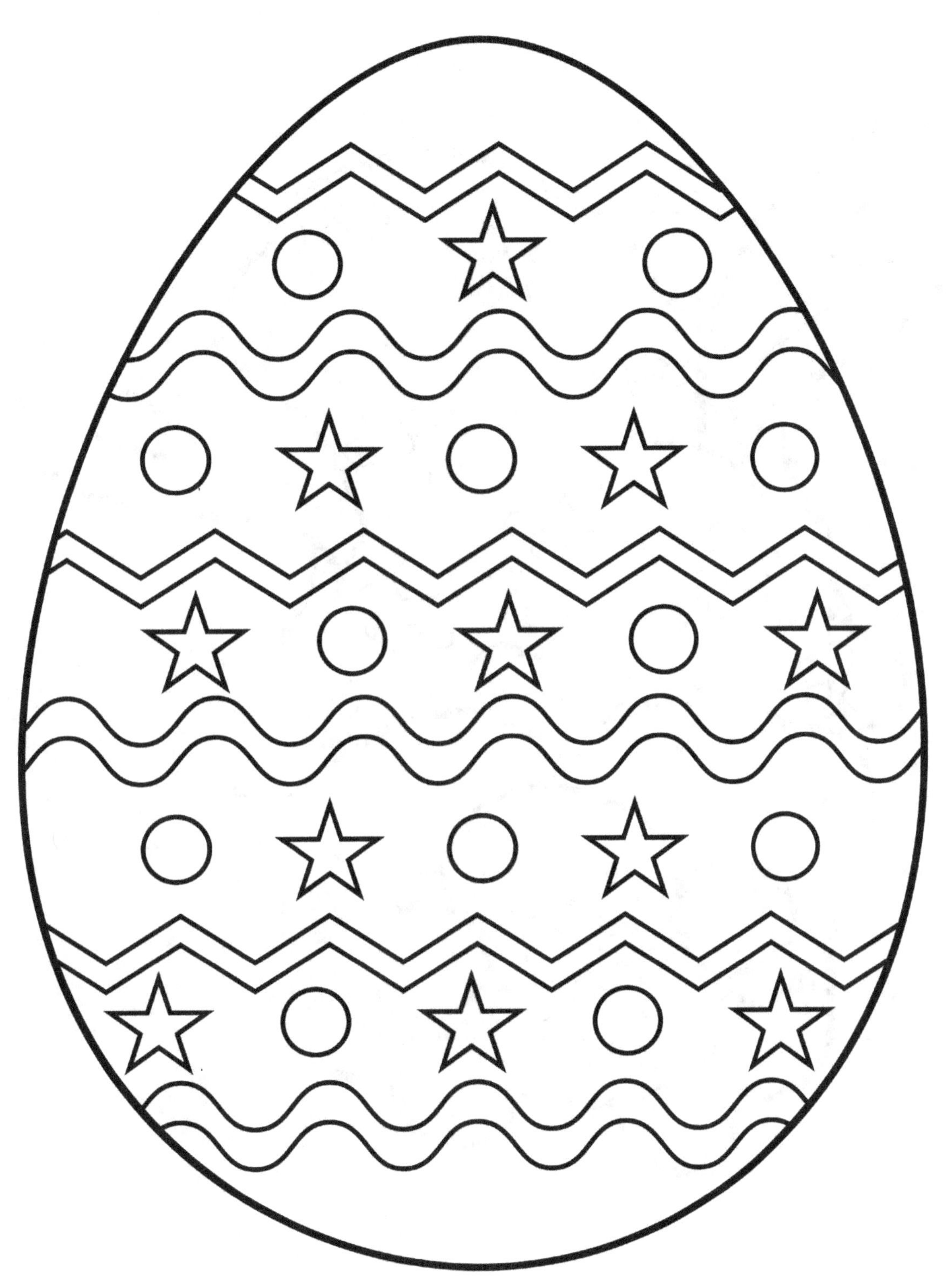

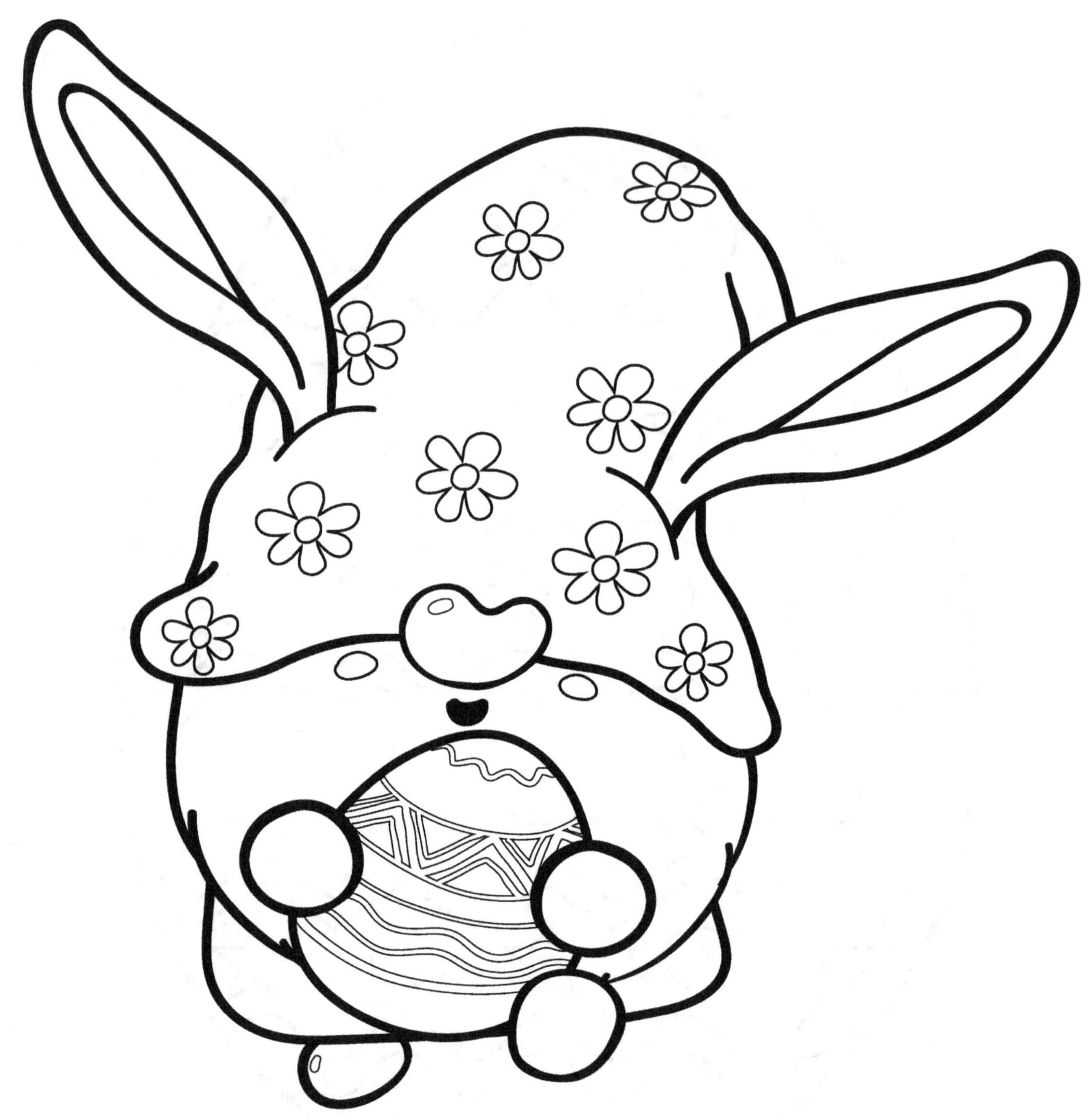

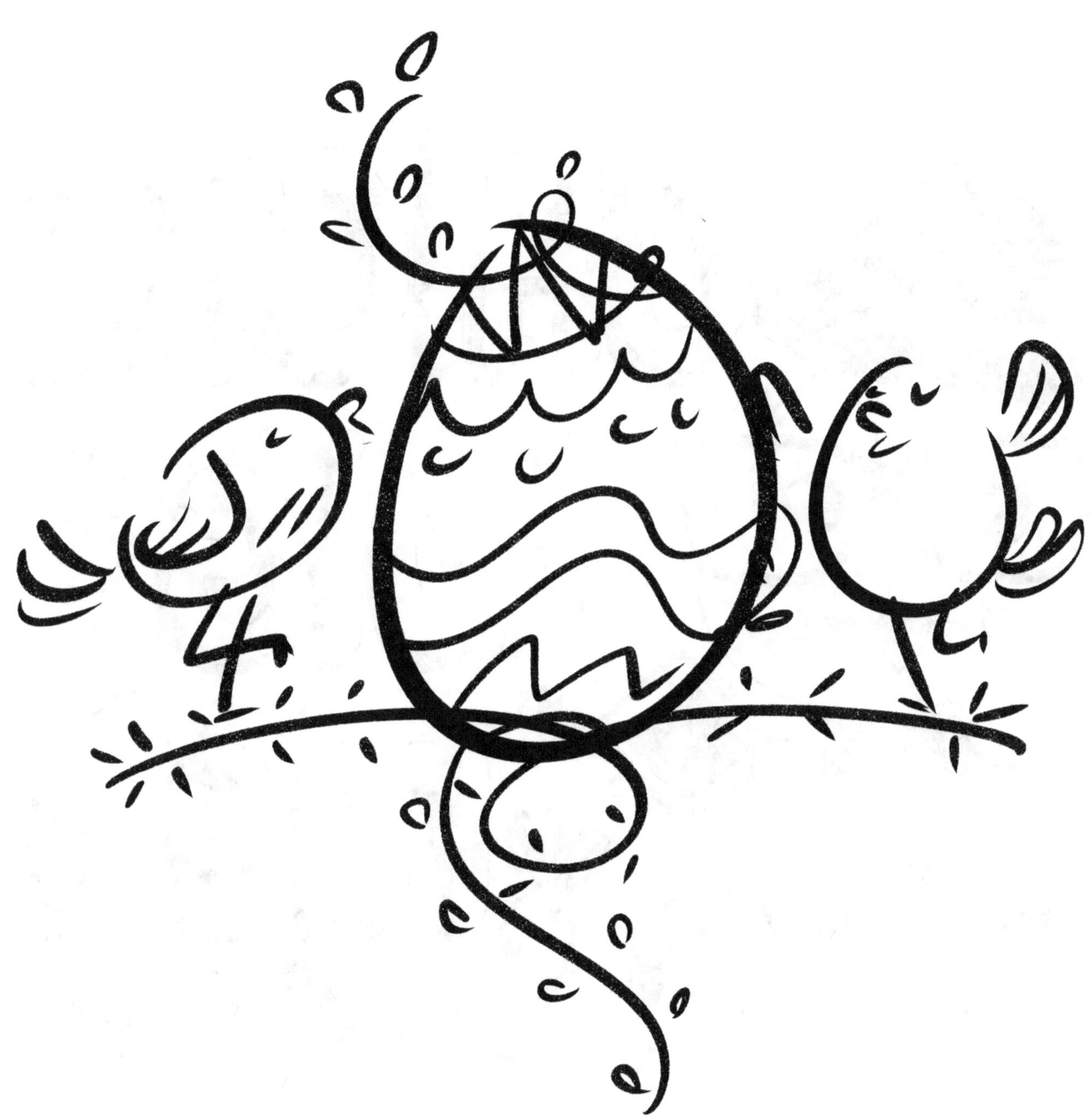

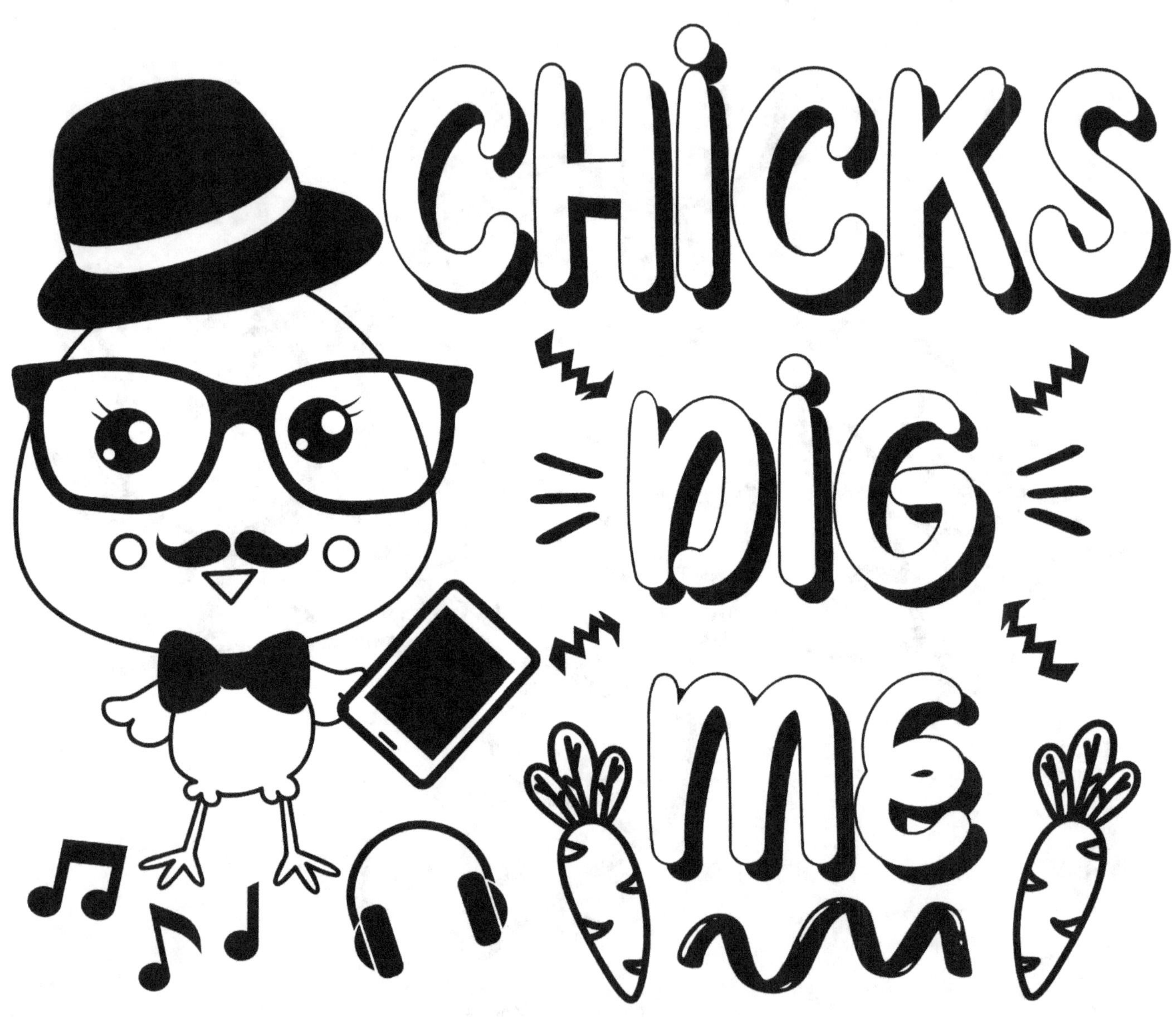
CHICKS
DIG
ME

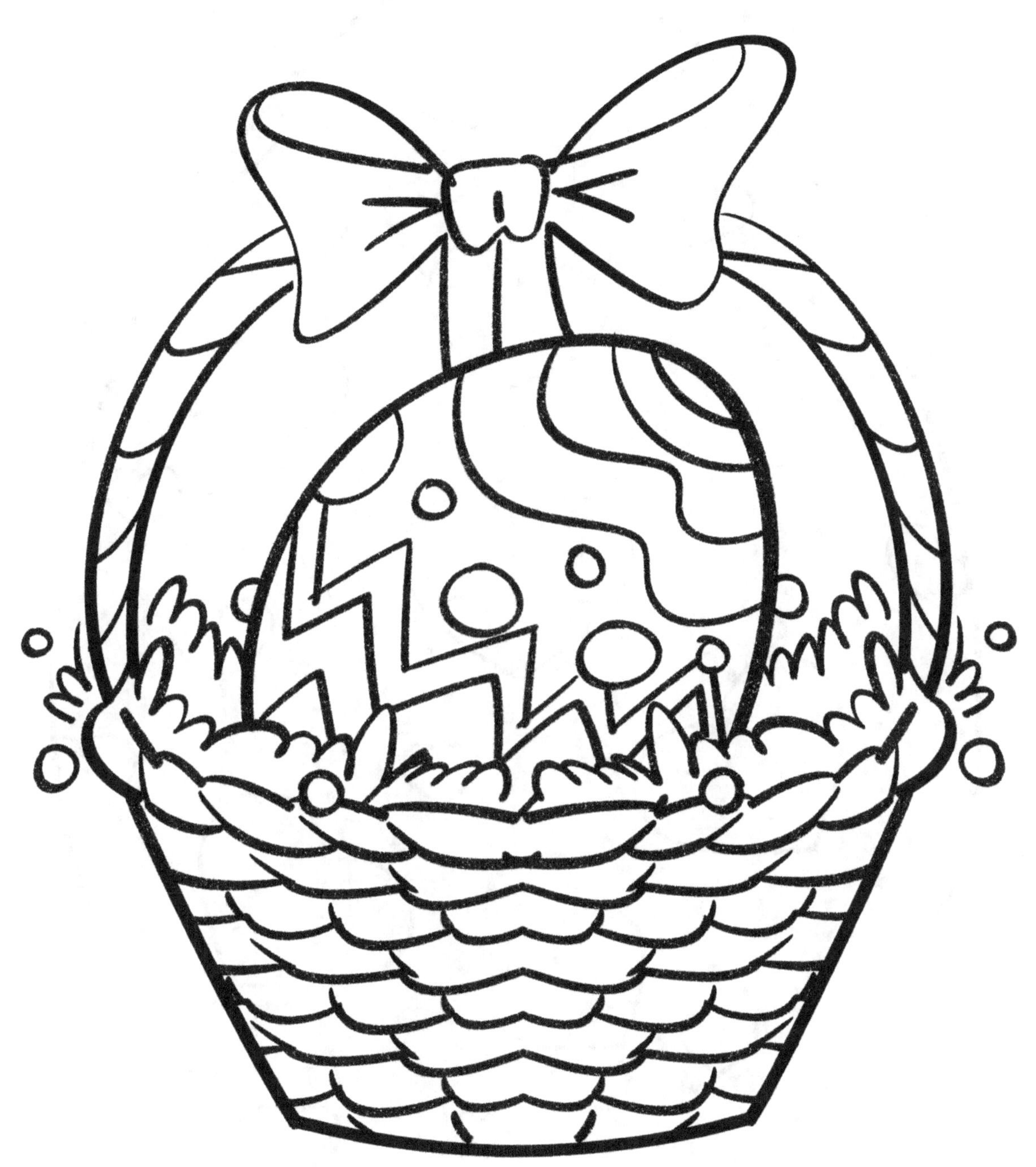

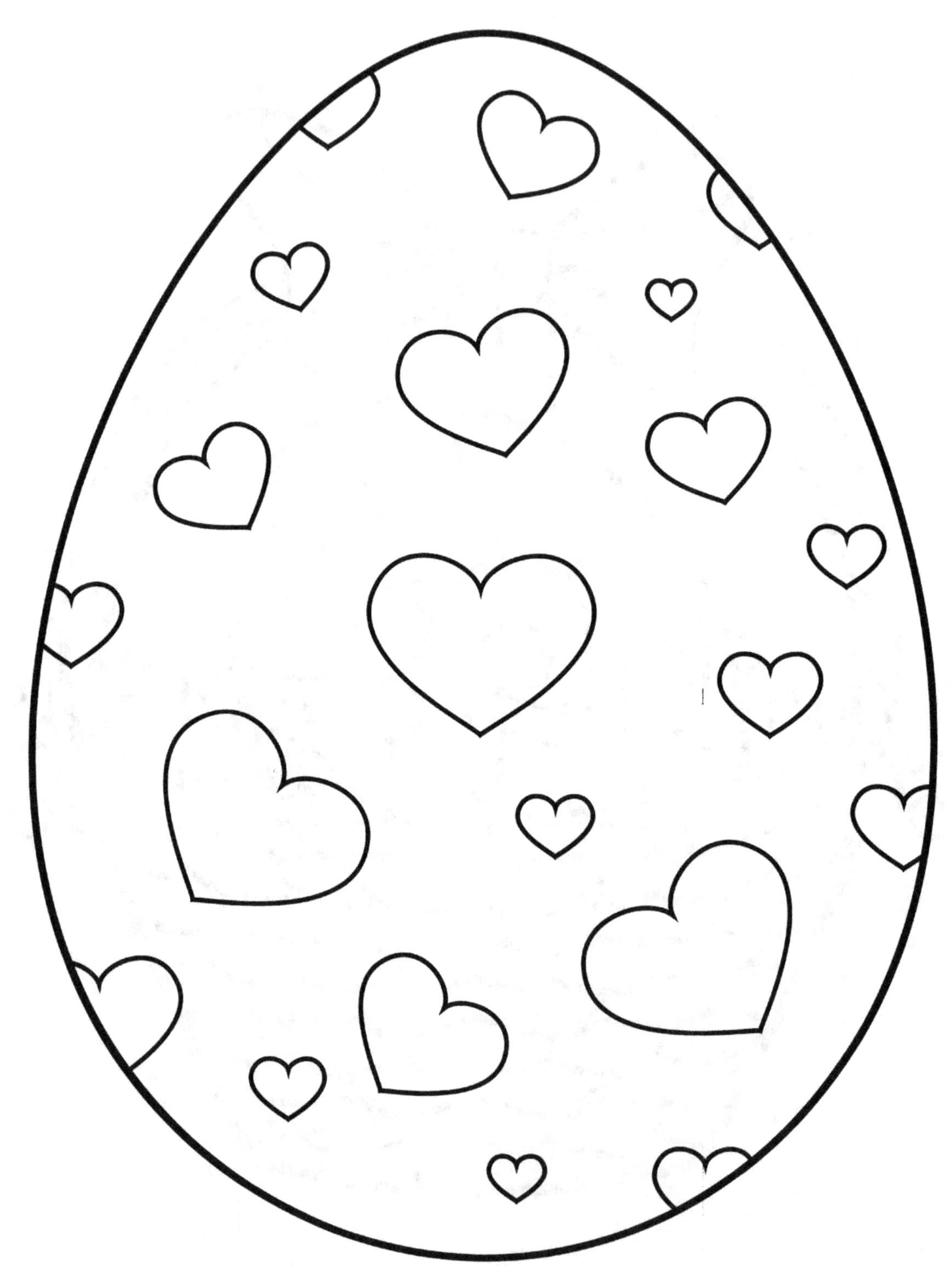

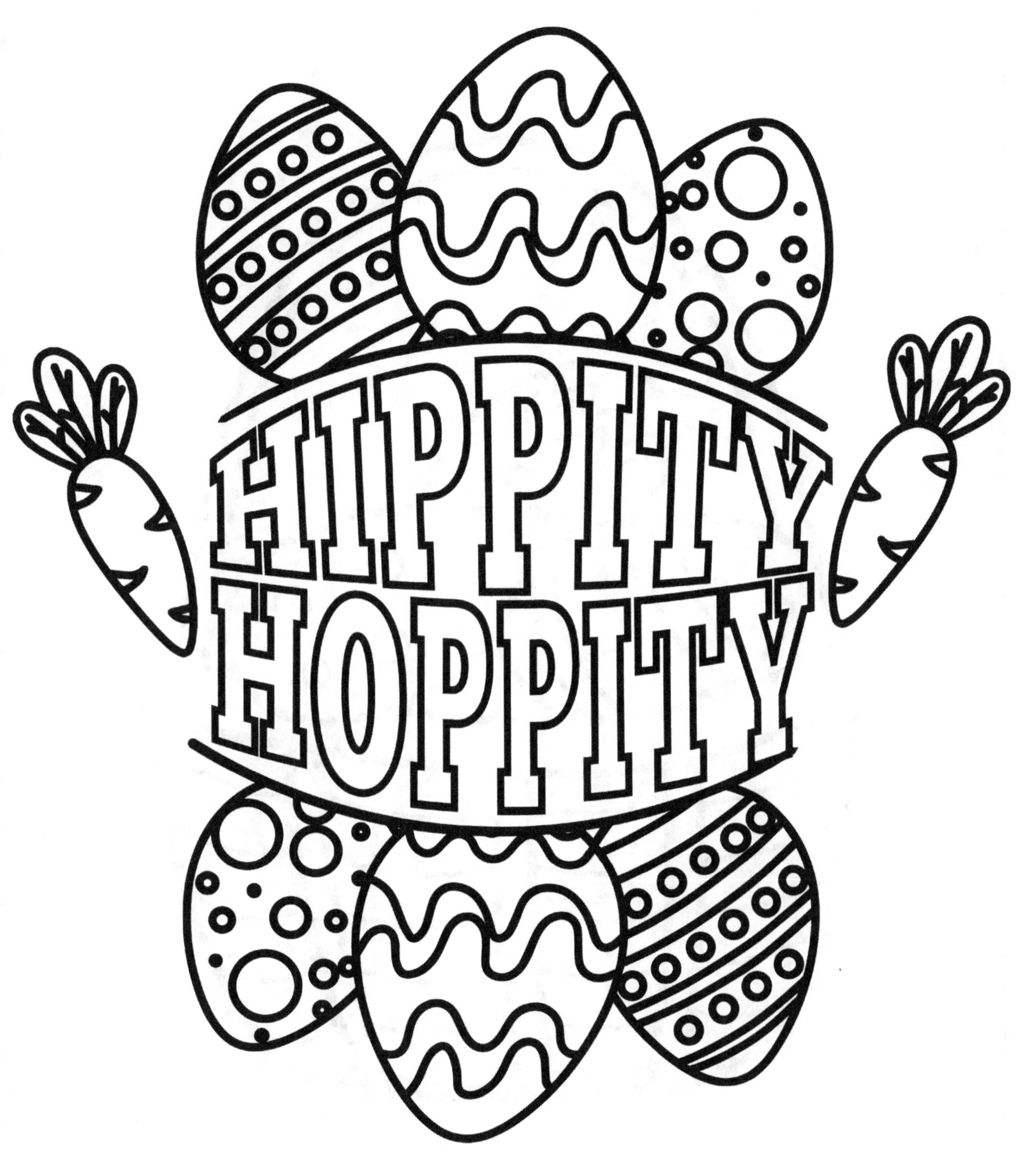

HIPPITY
HOPPITY

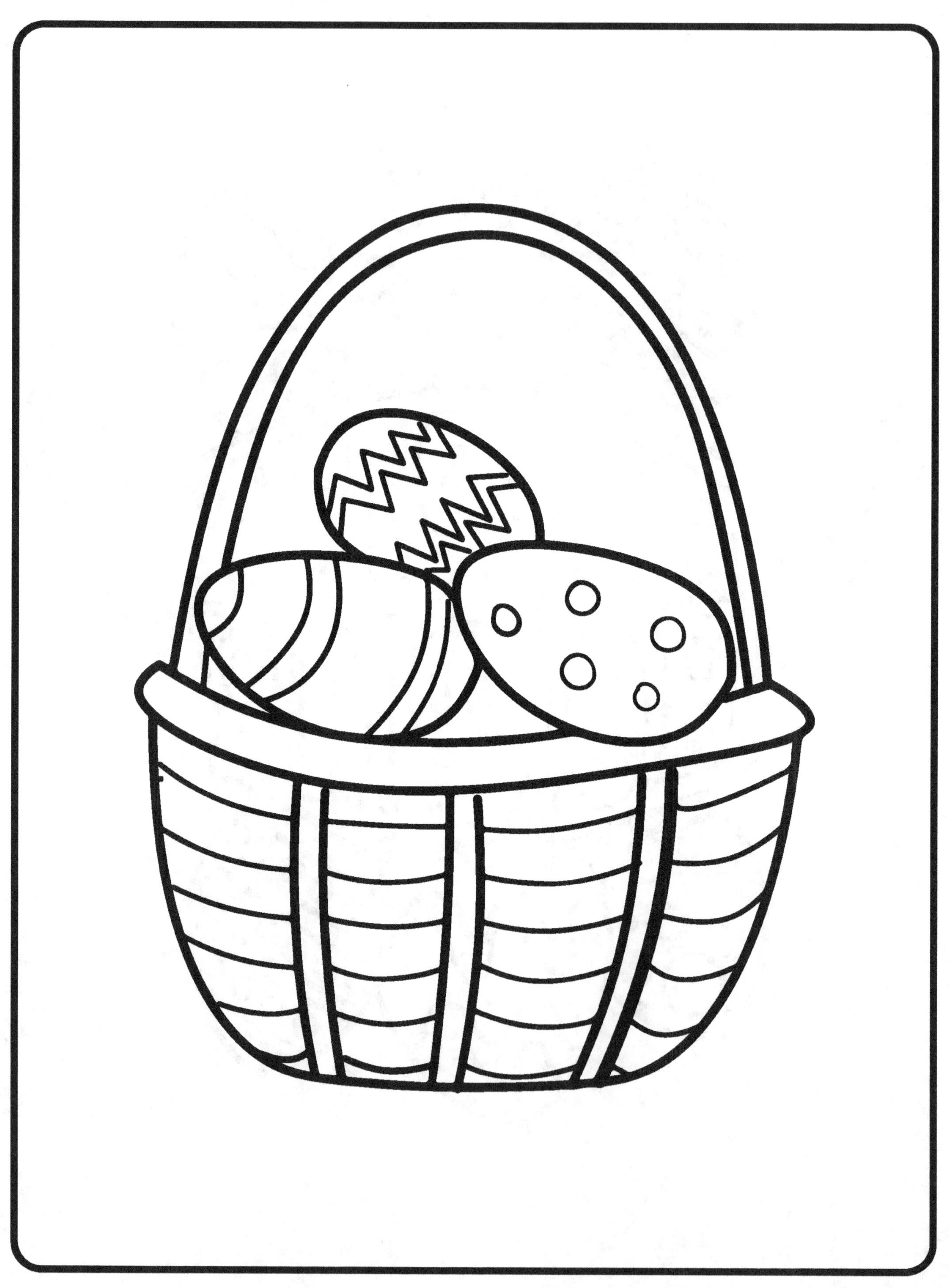

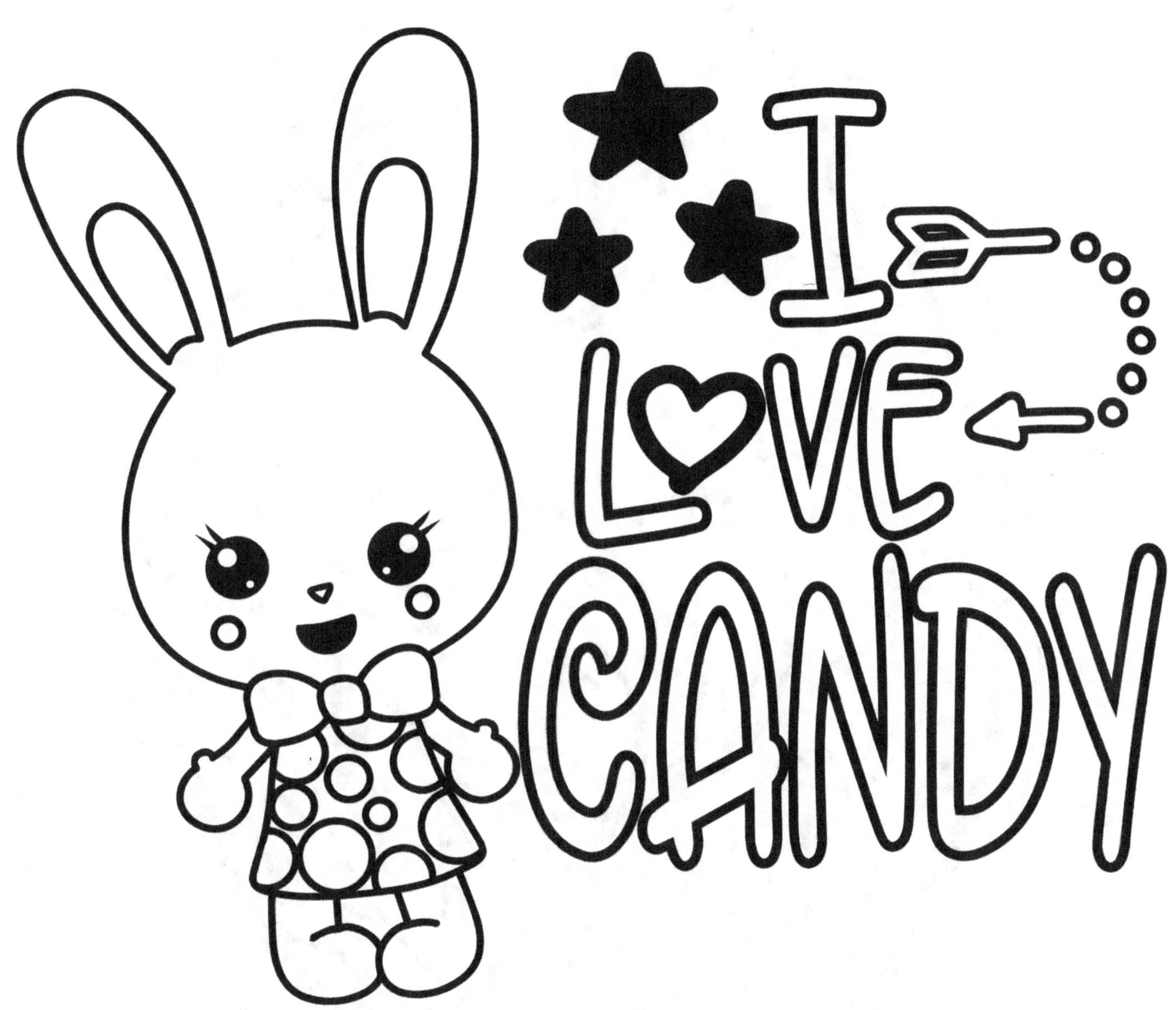
I
LOVE
CANDY

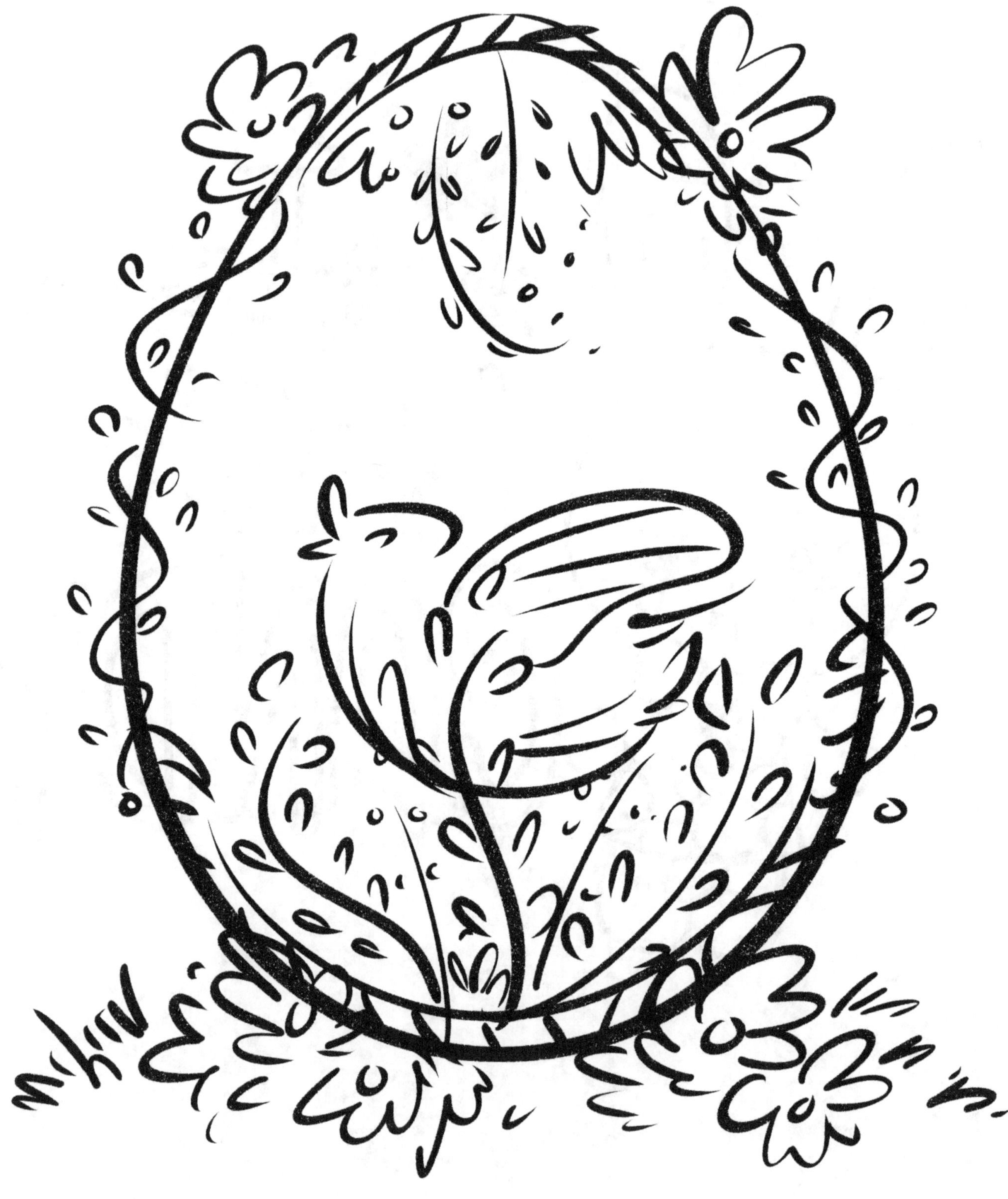

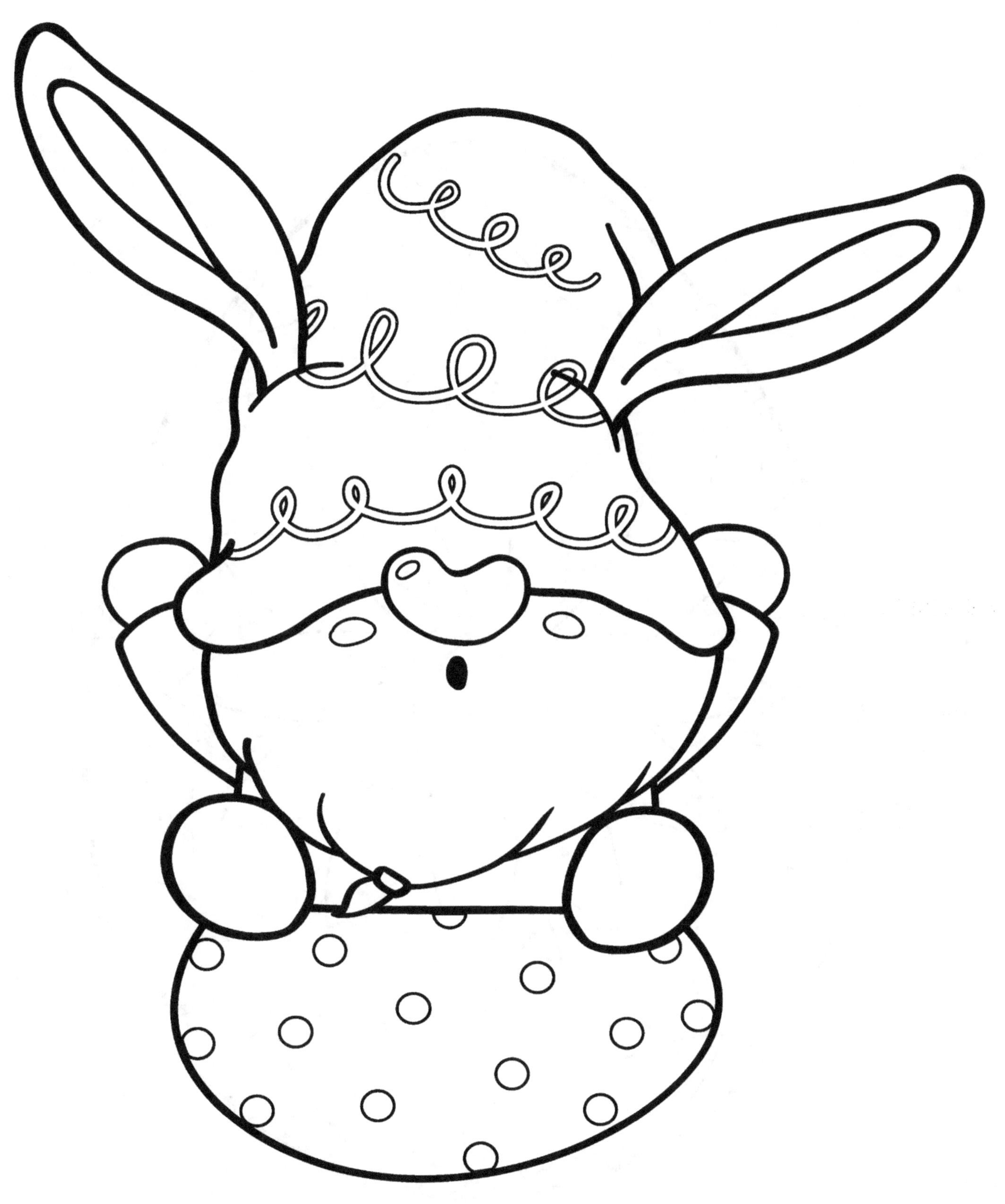

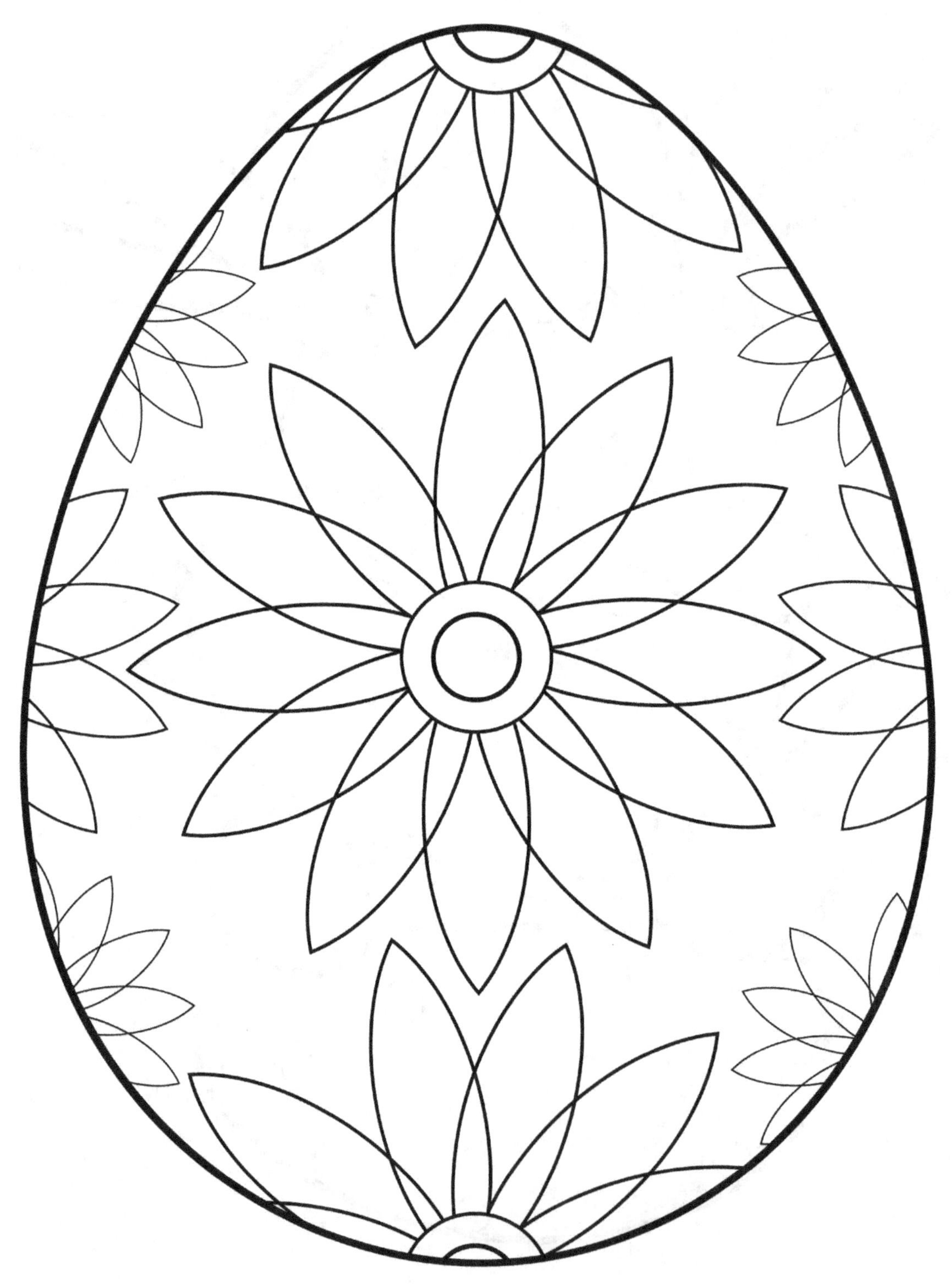

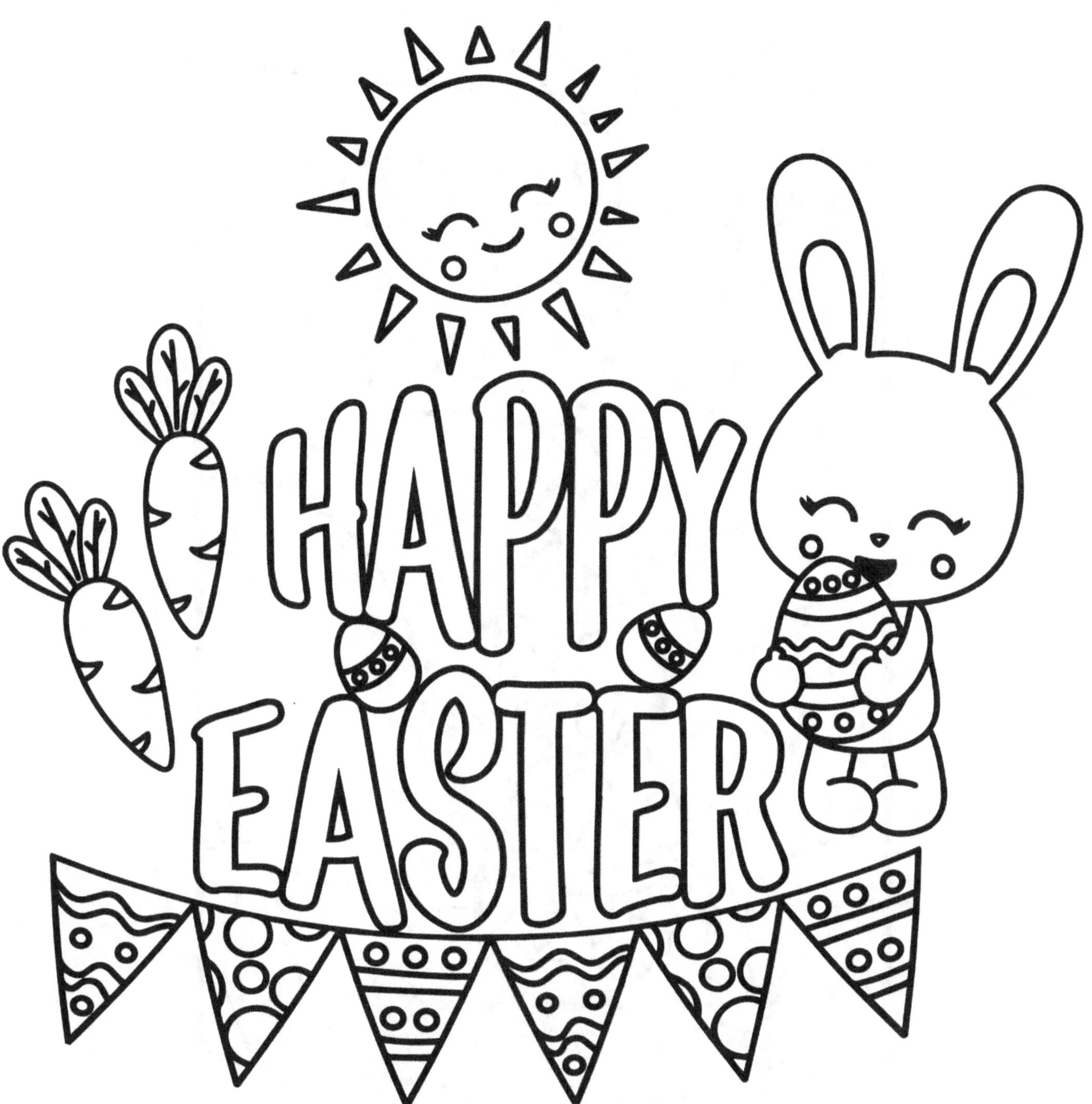

HAPPY
EASTER

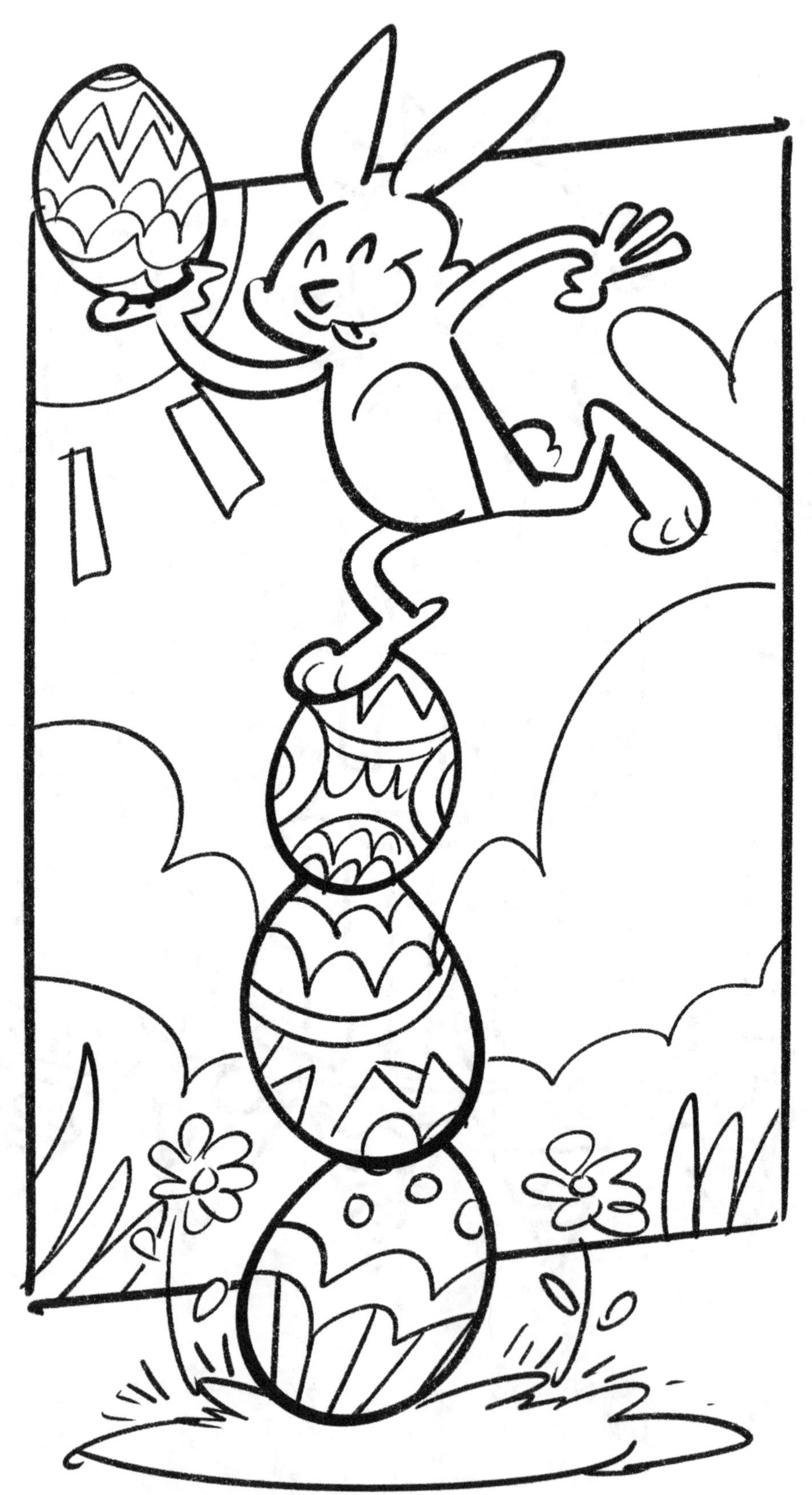

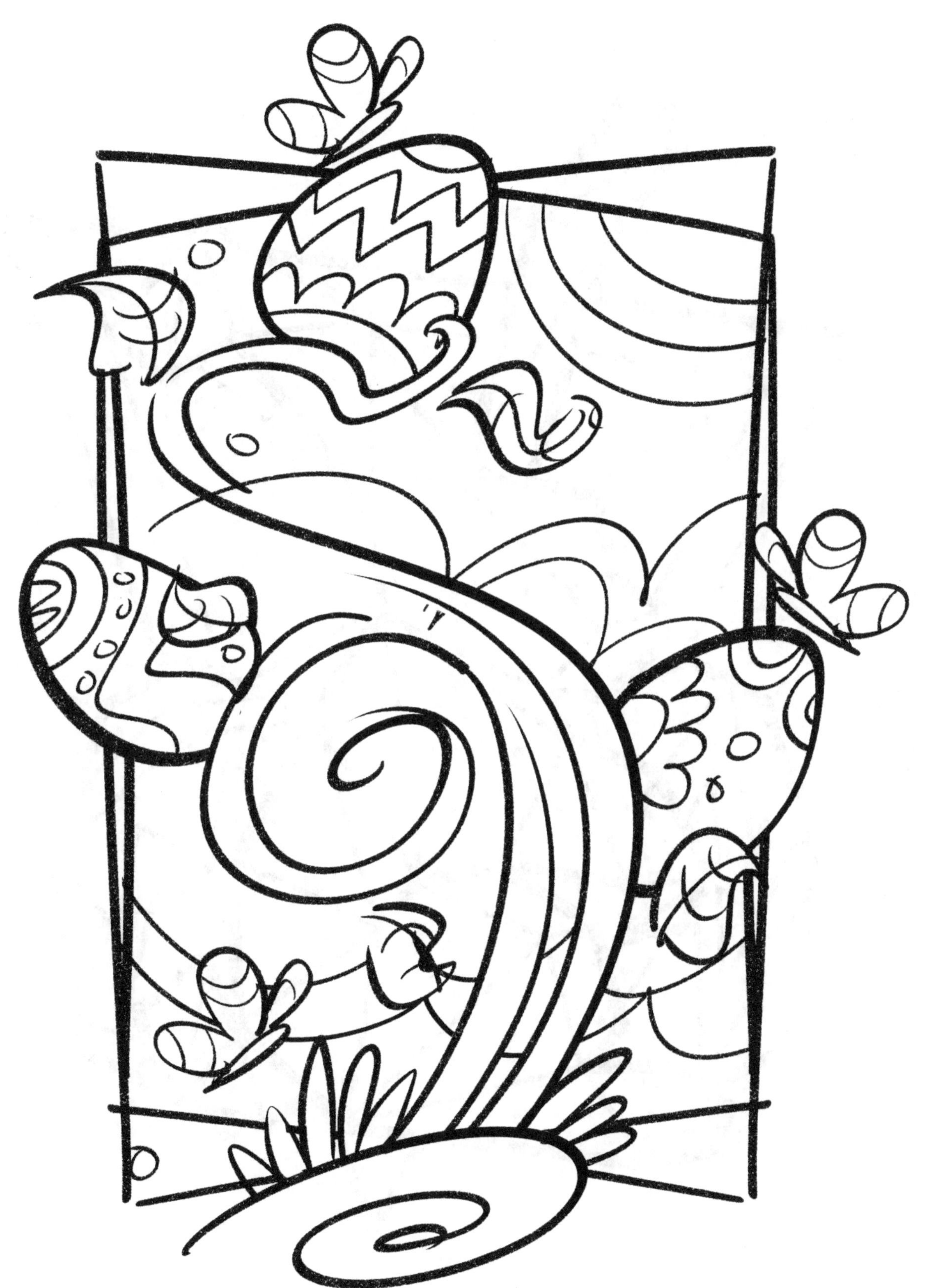

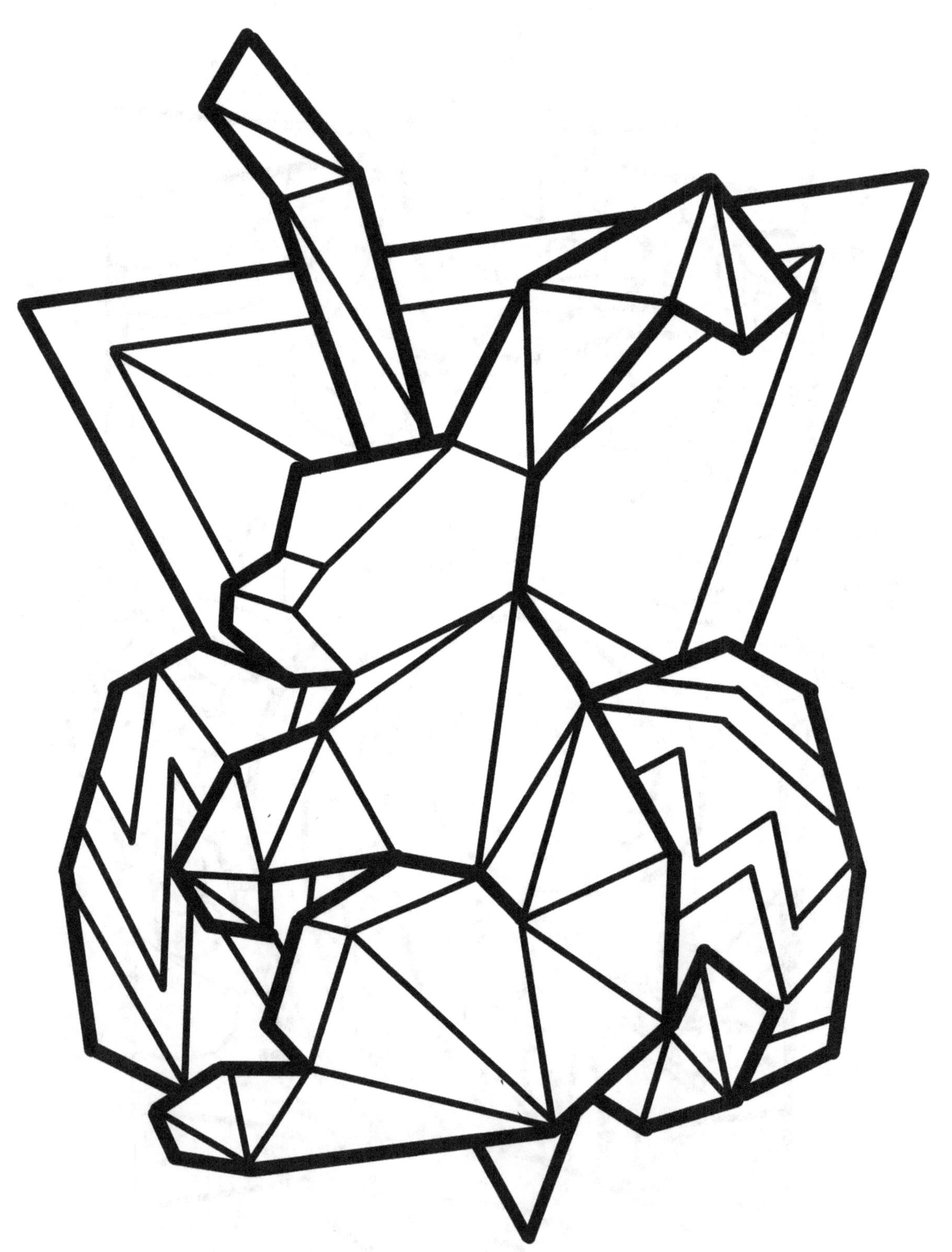

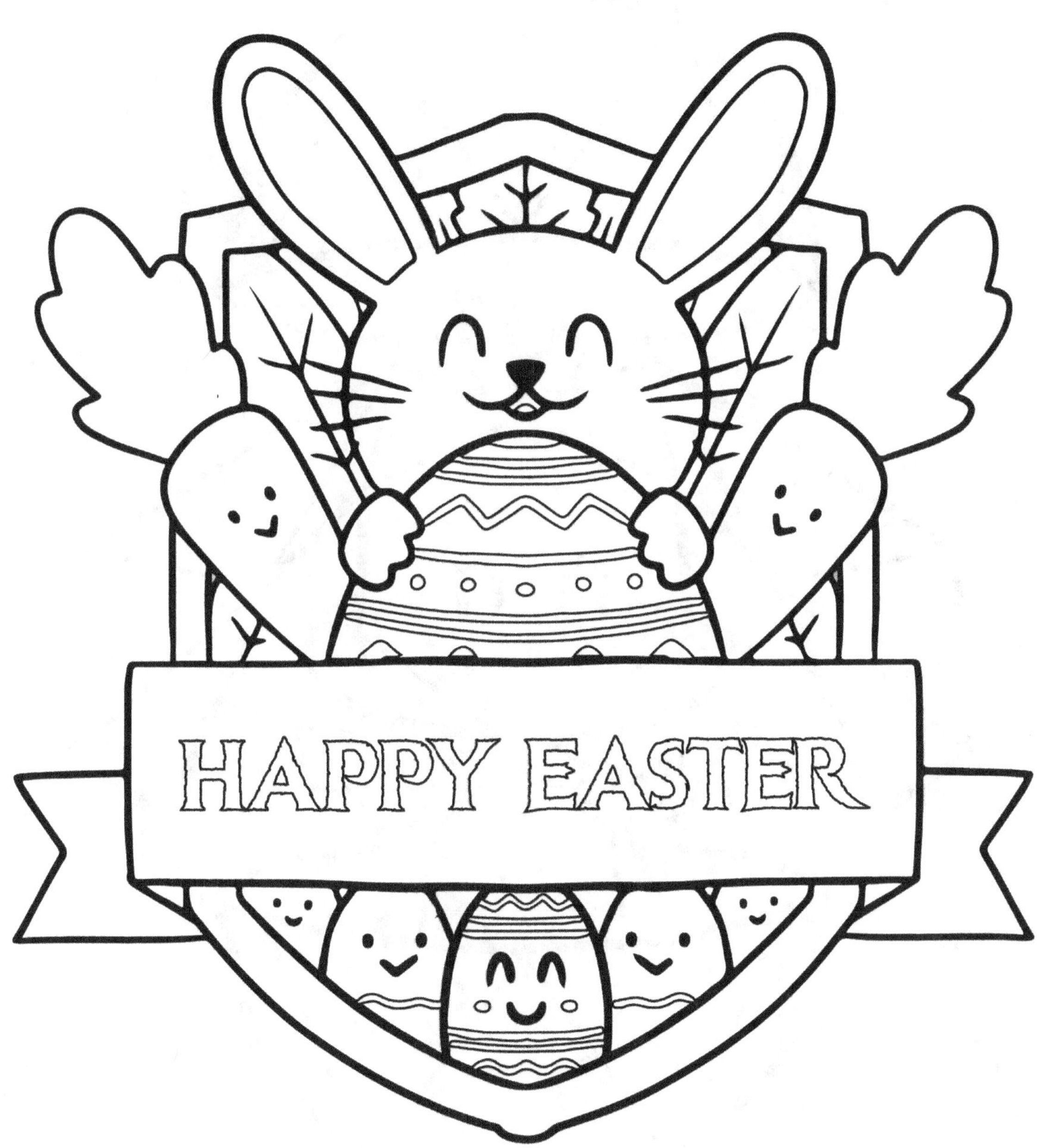
HAPPY EASTER

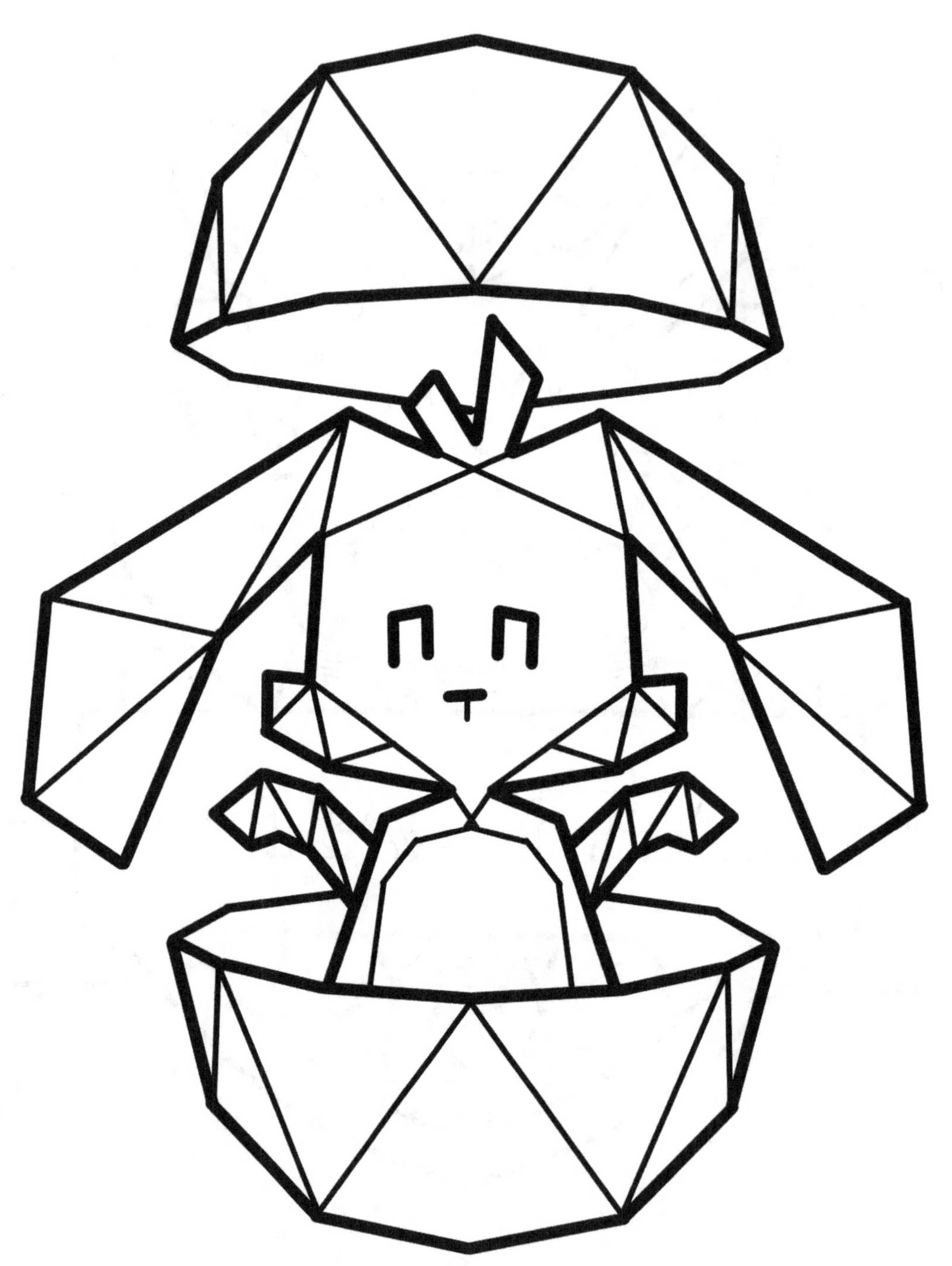

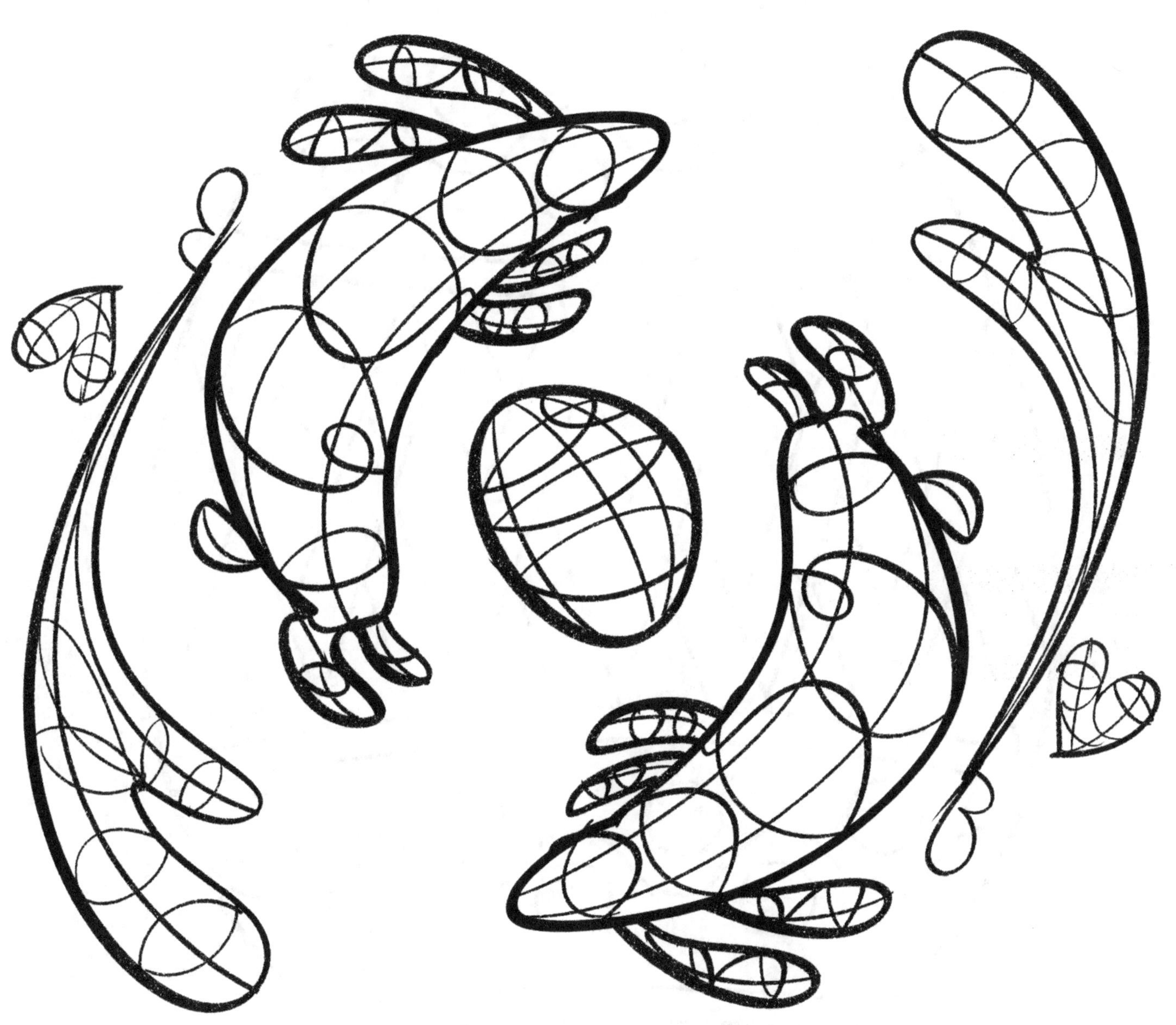

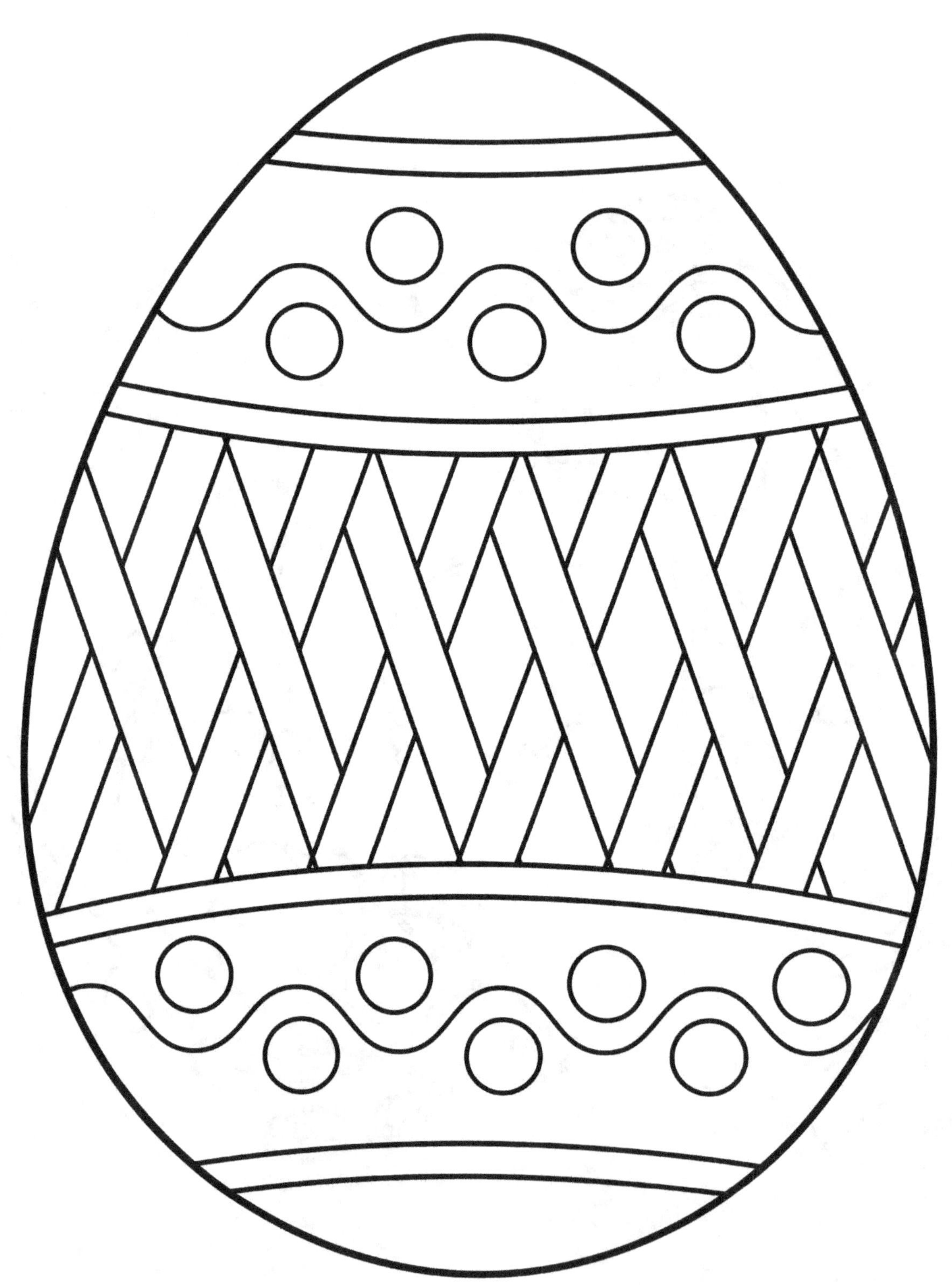

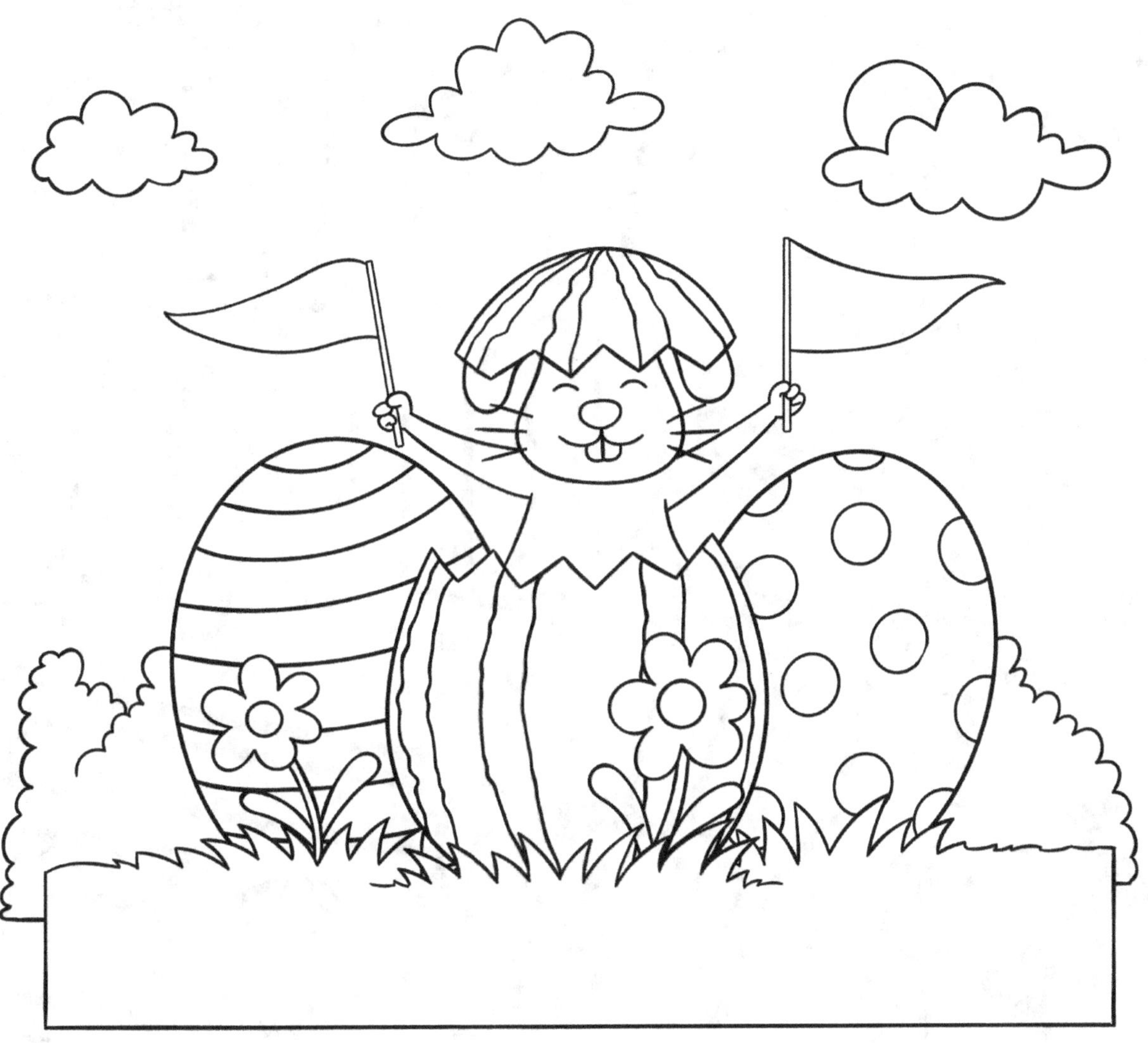

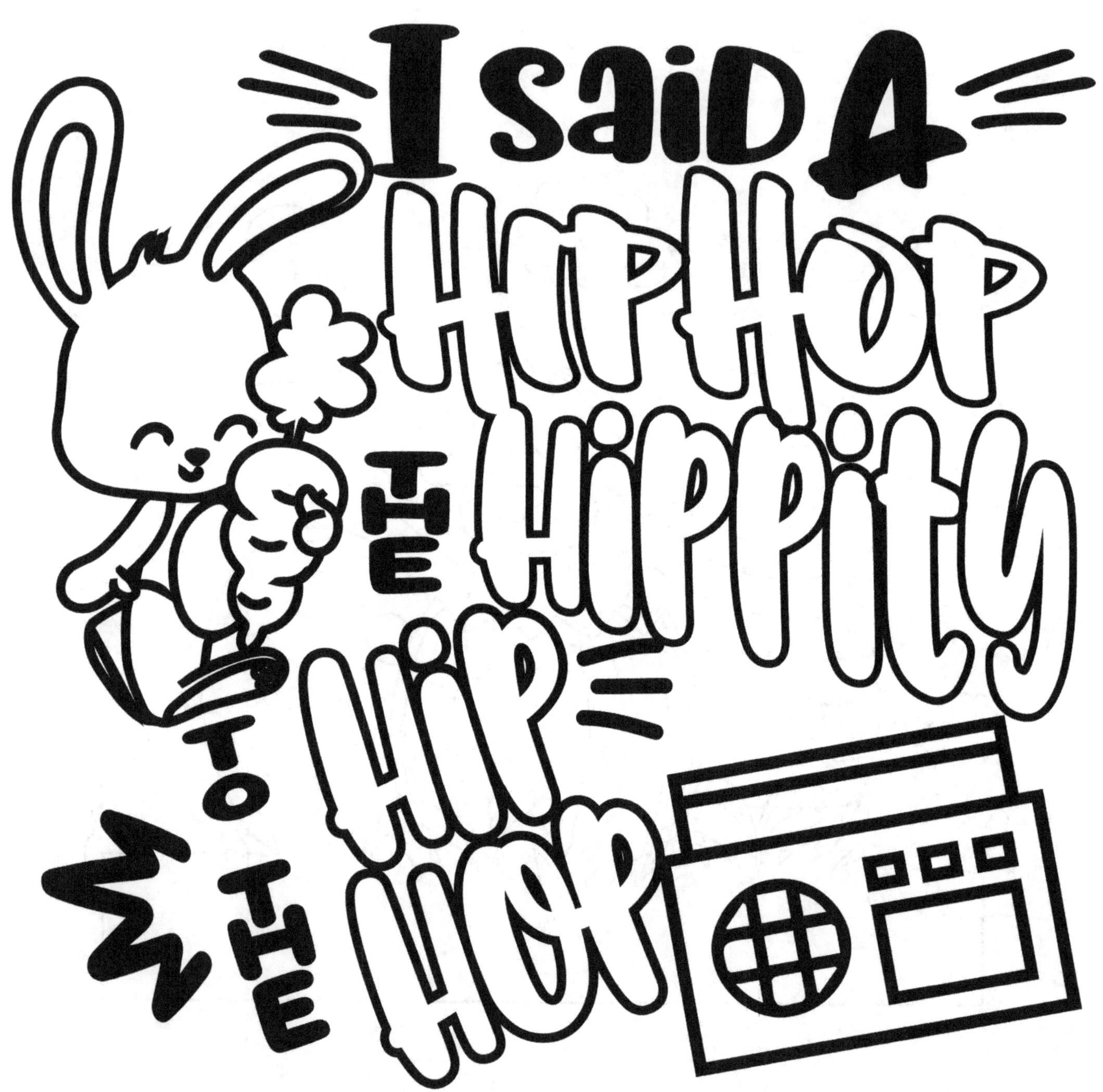

I SAID A
HIP HOP
THE HIPPITY
TO THE HIP
HOP

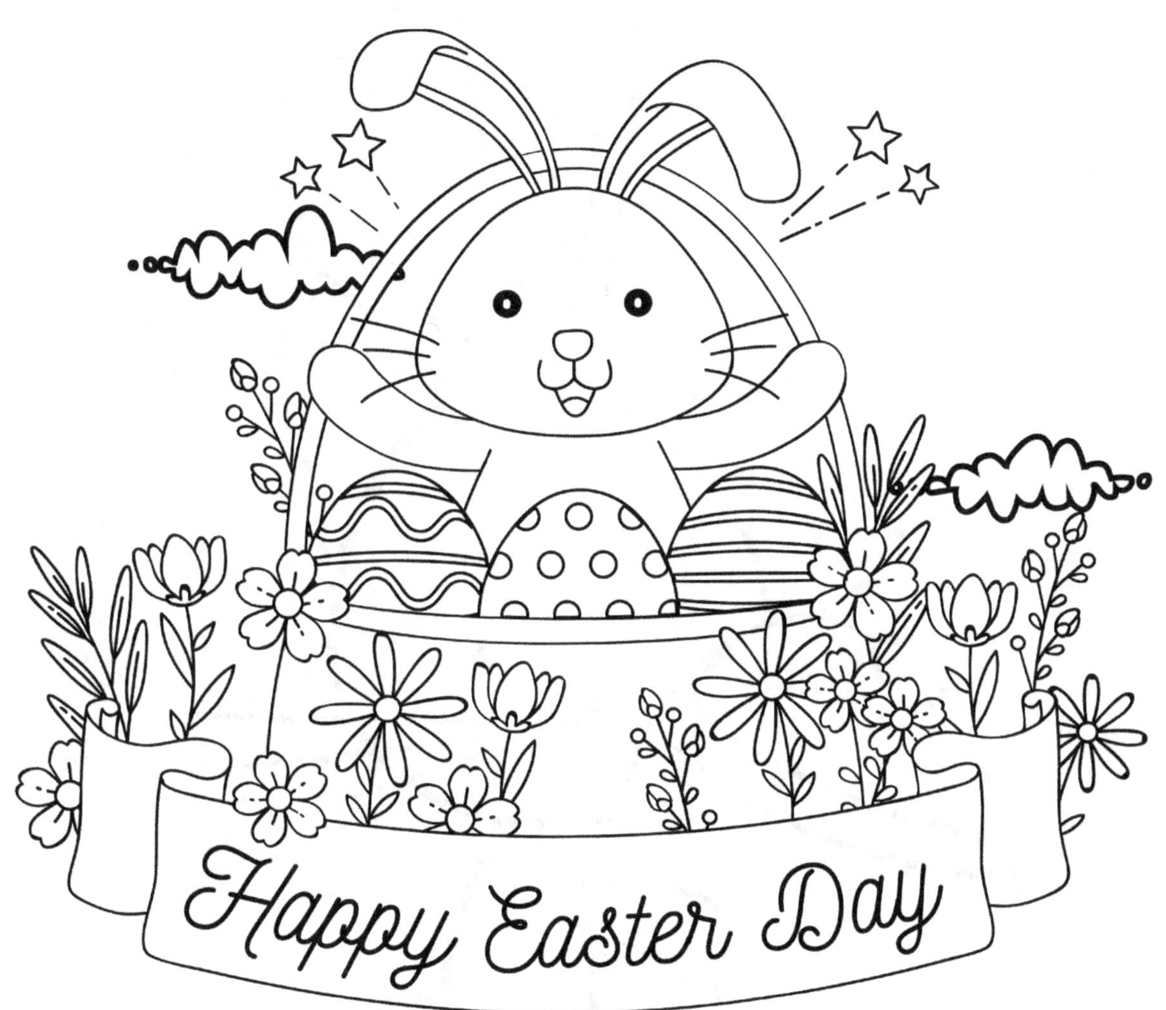
Happy Easter Day

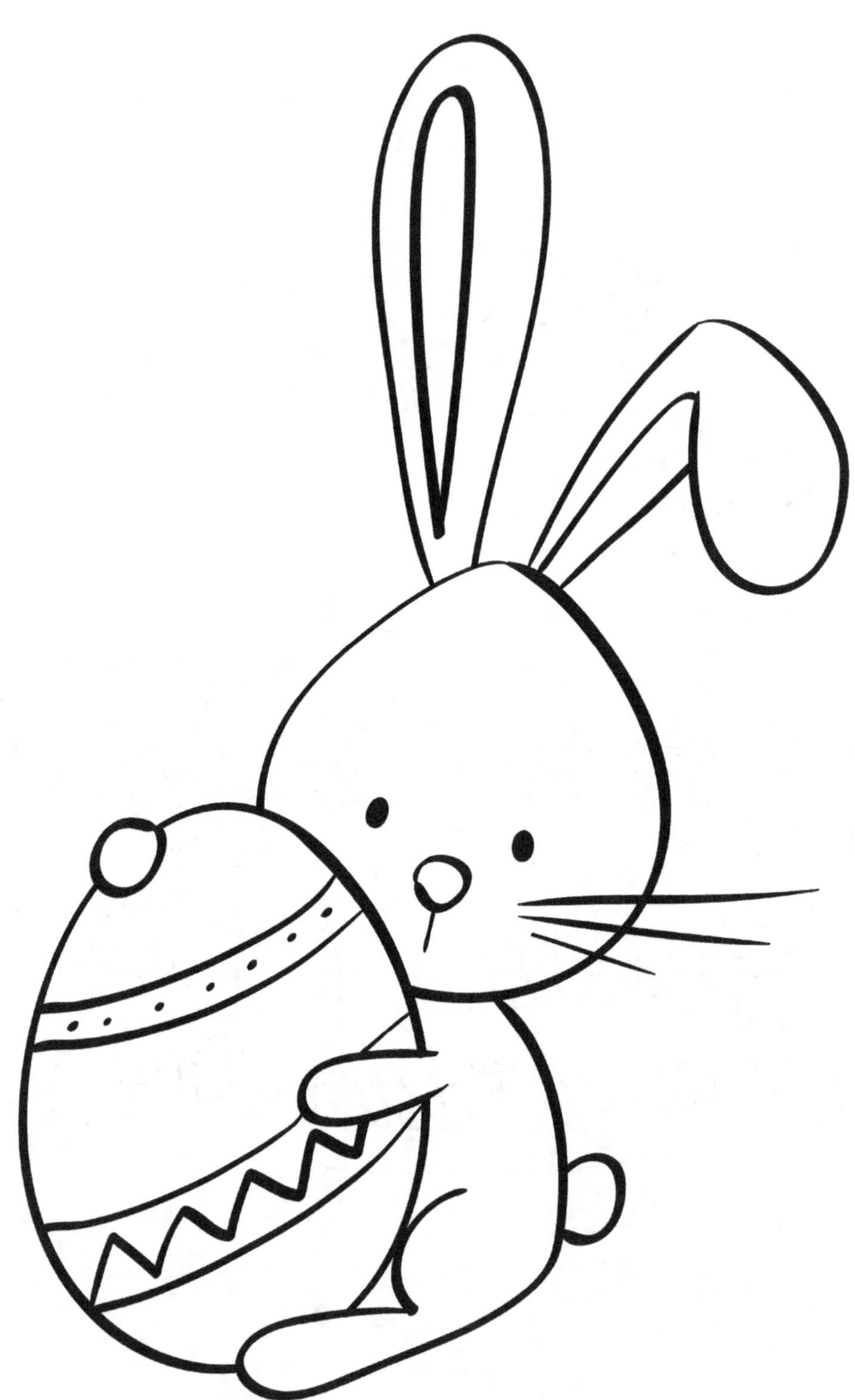

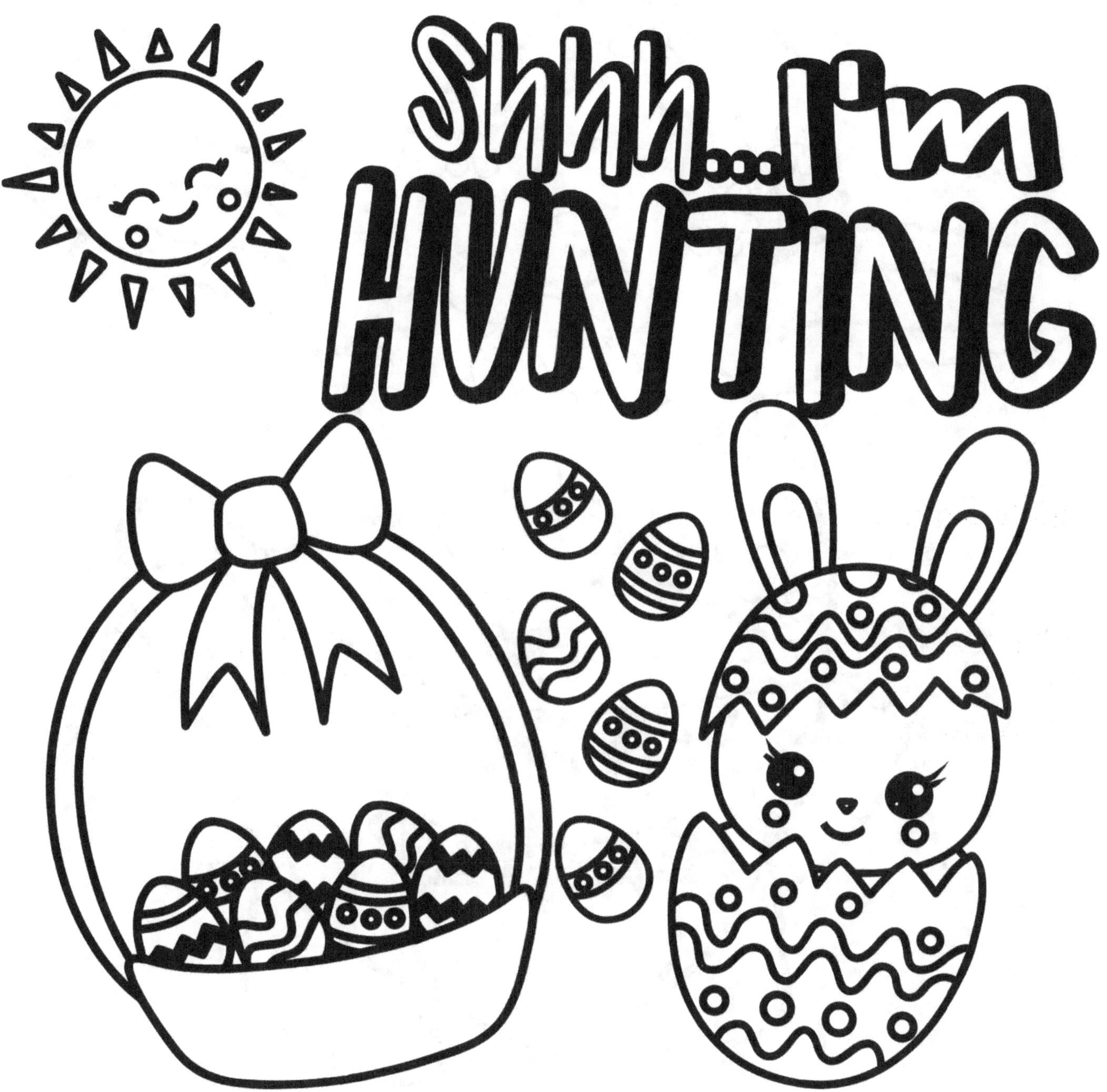

Shhh...I'm HUNTING

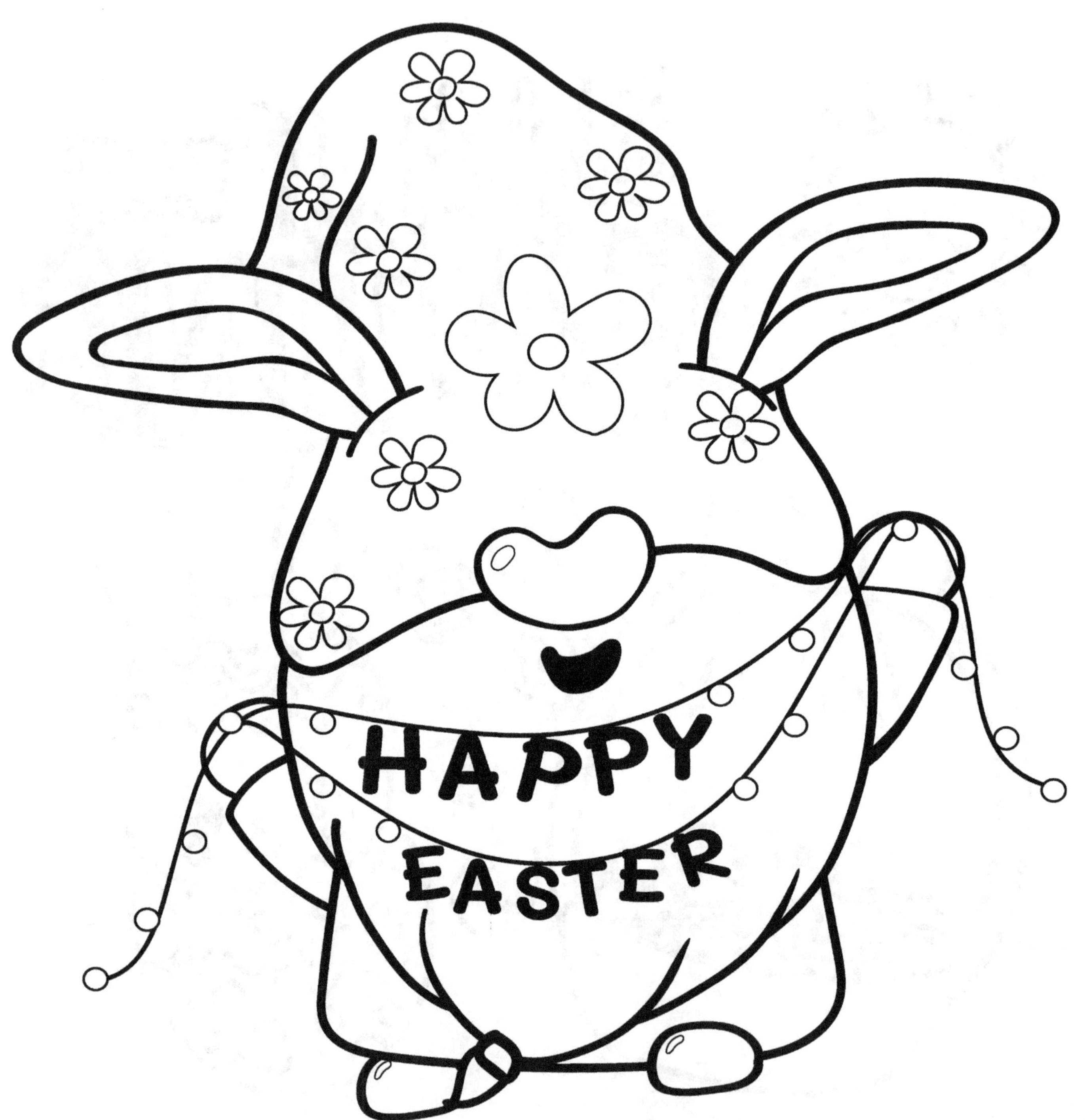

HAPPY
EASTER

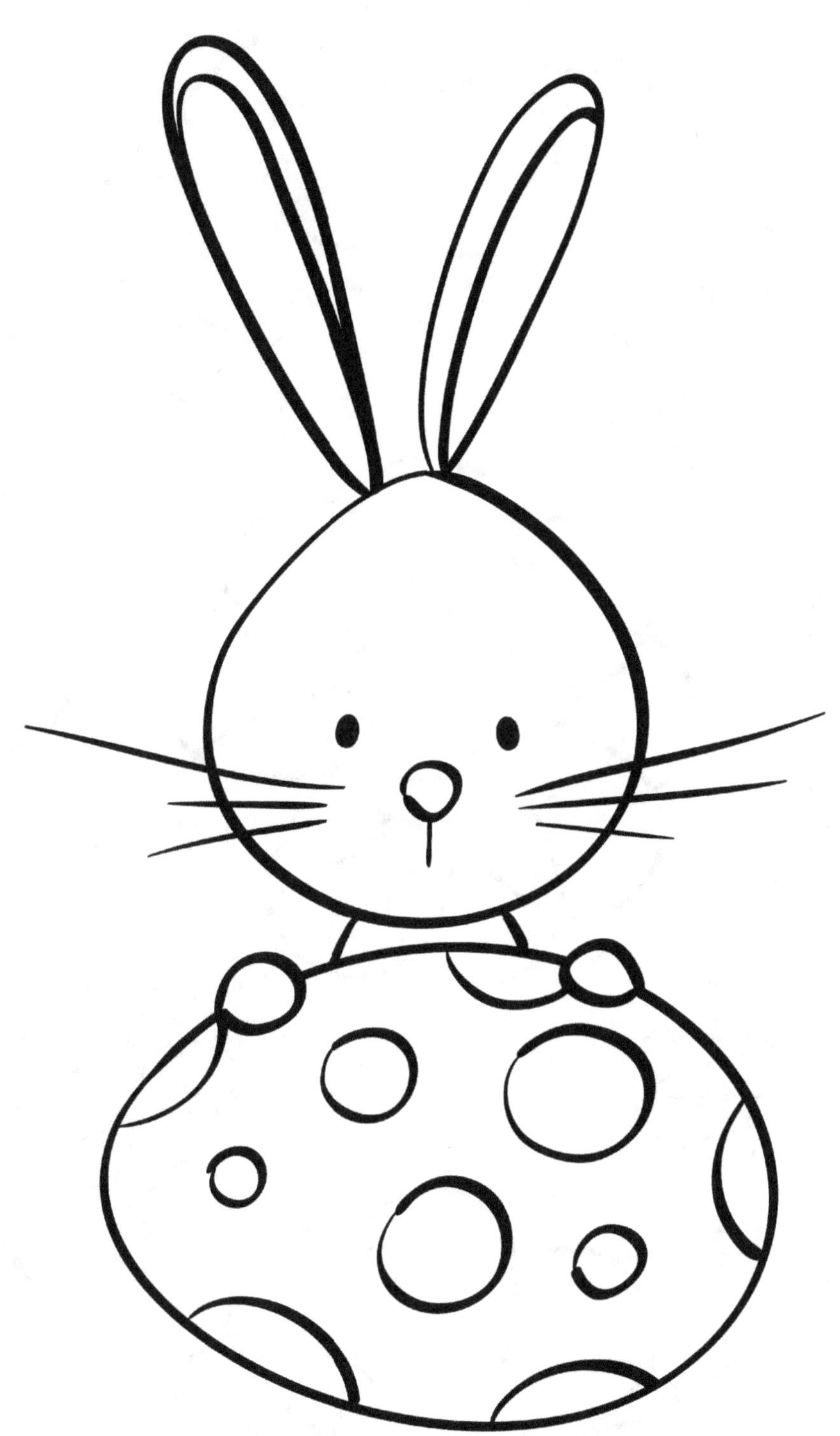

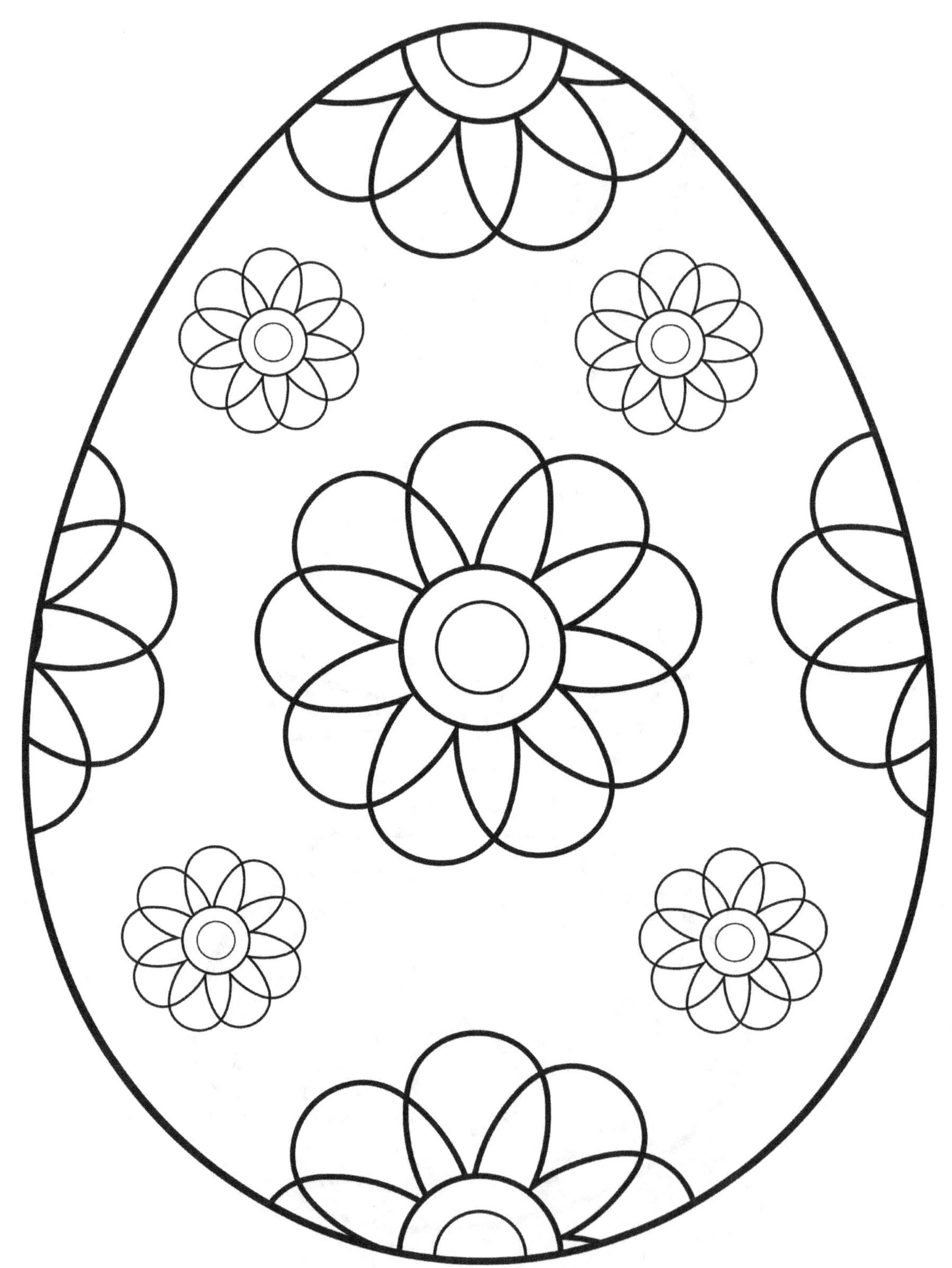

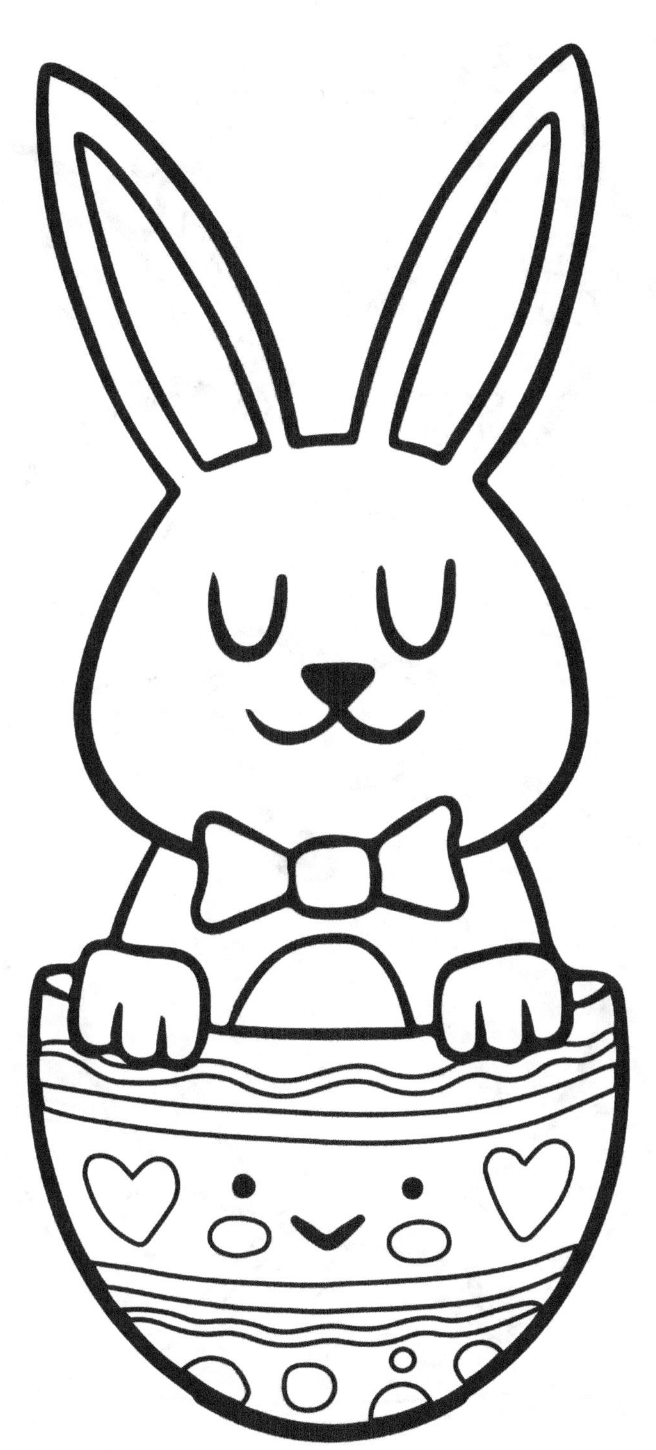

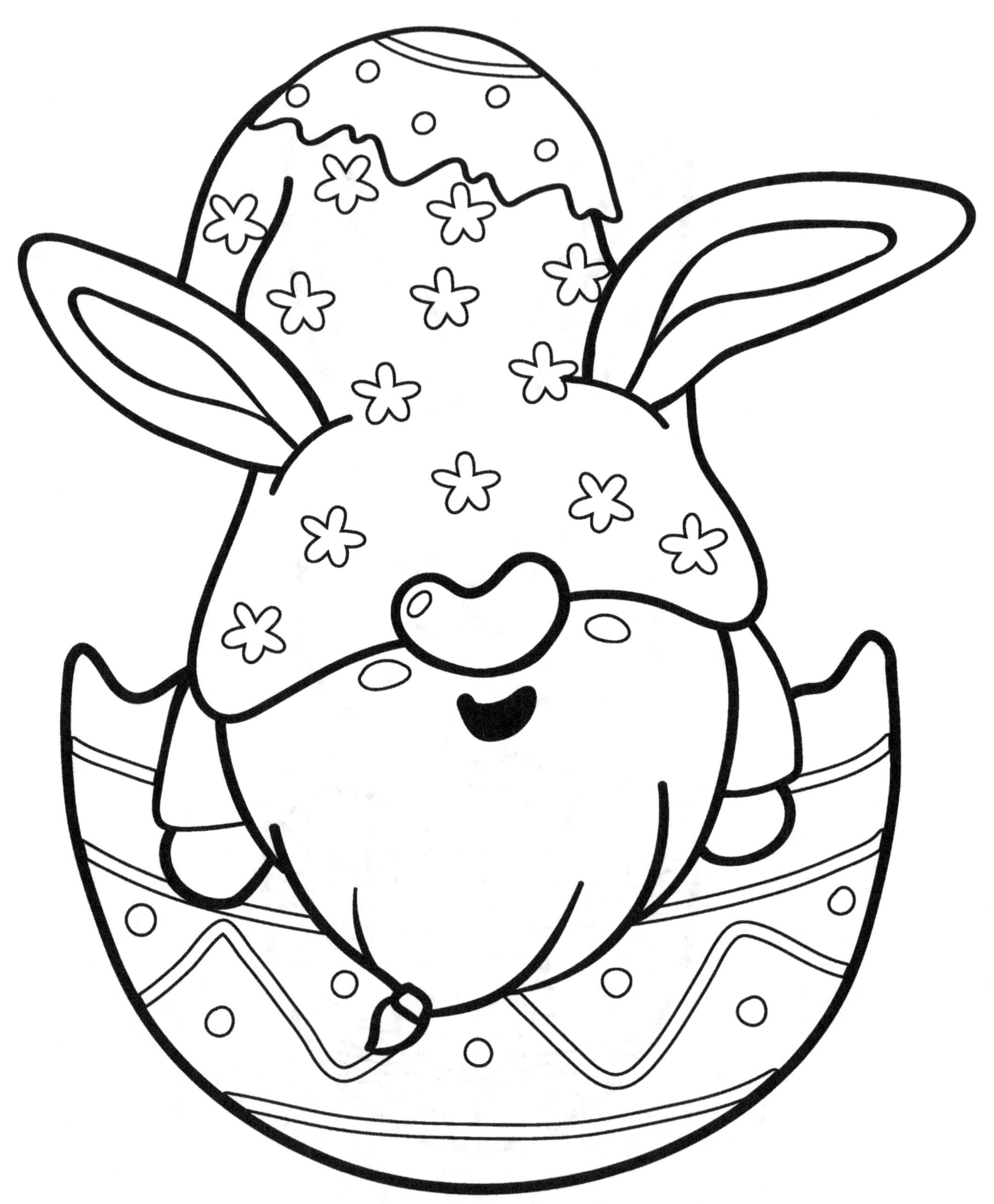

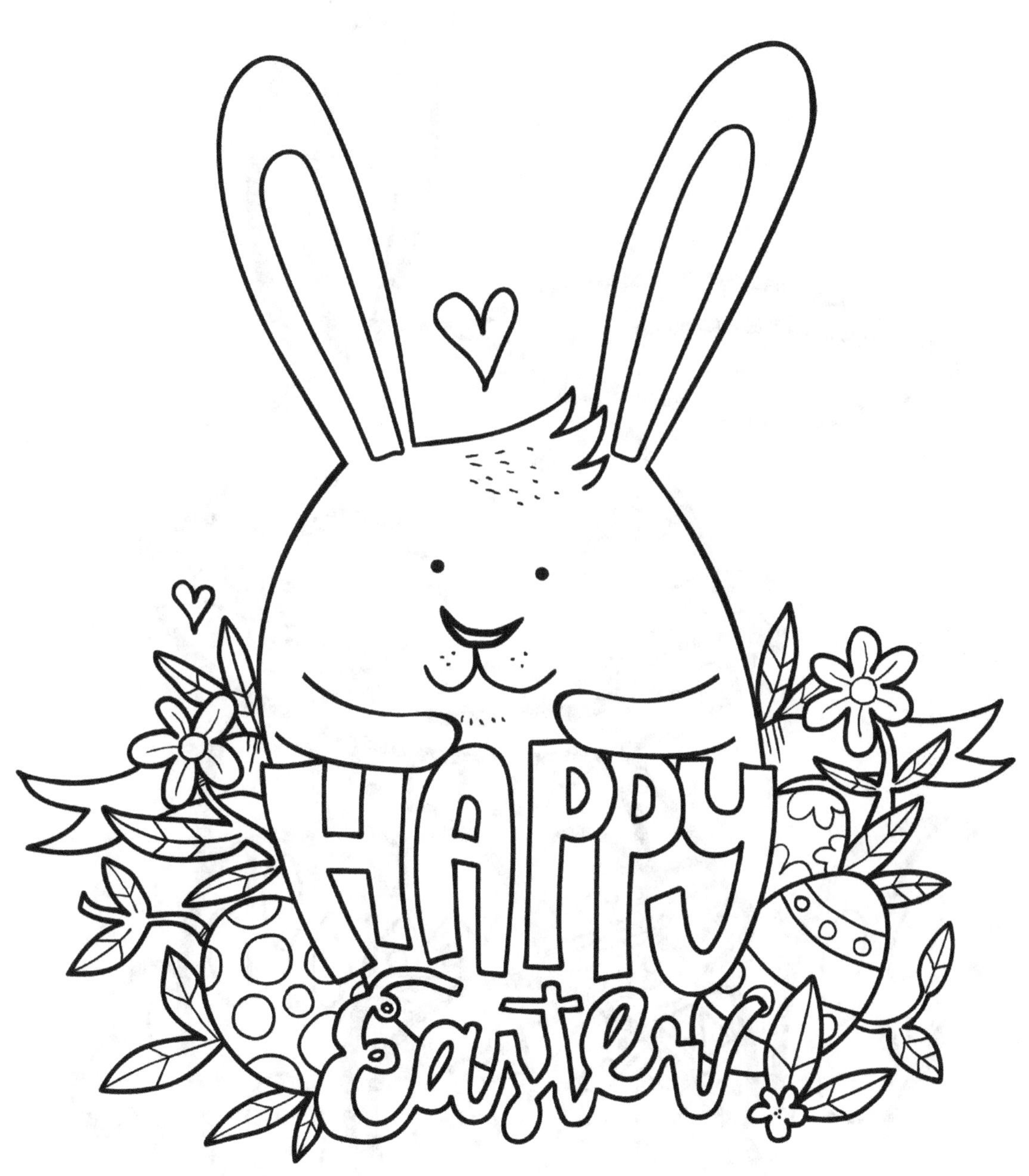
HAPPY
Easter

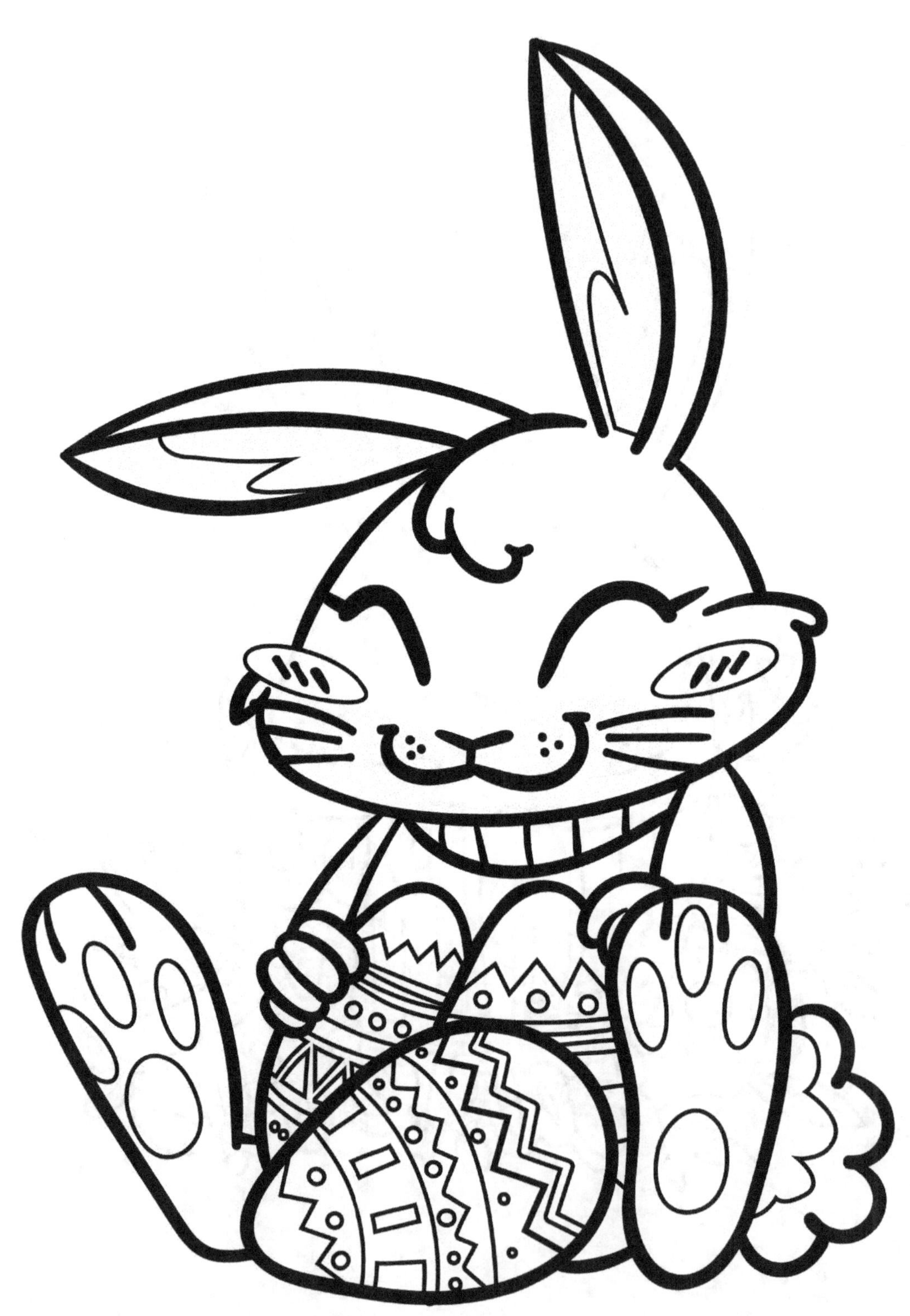

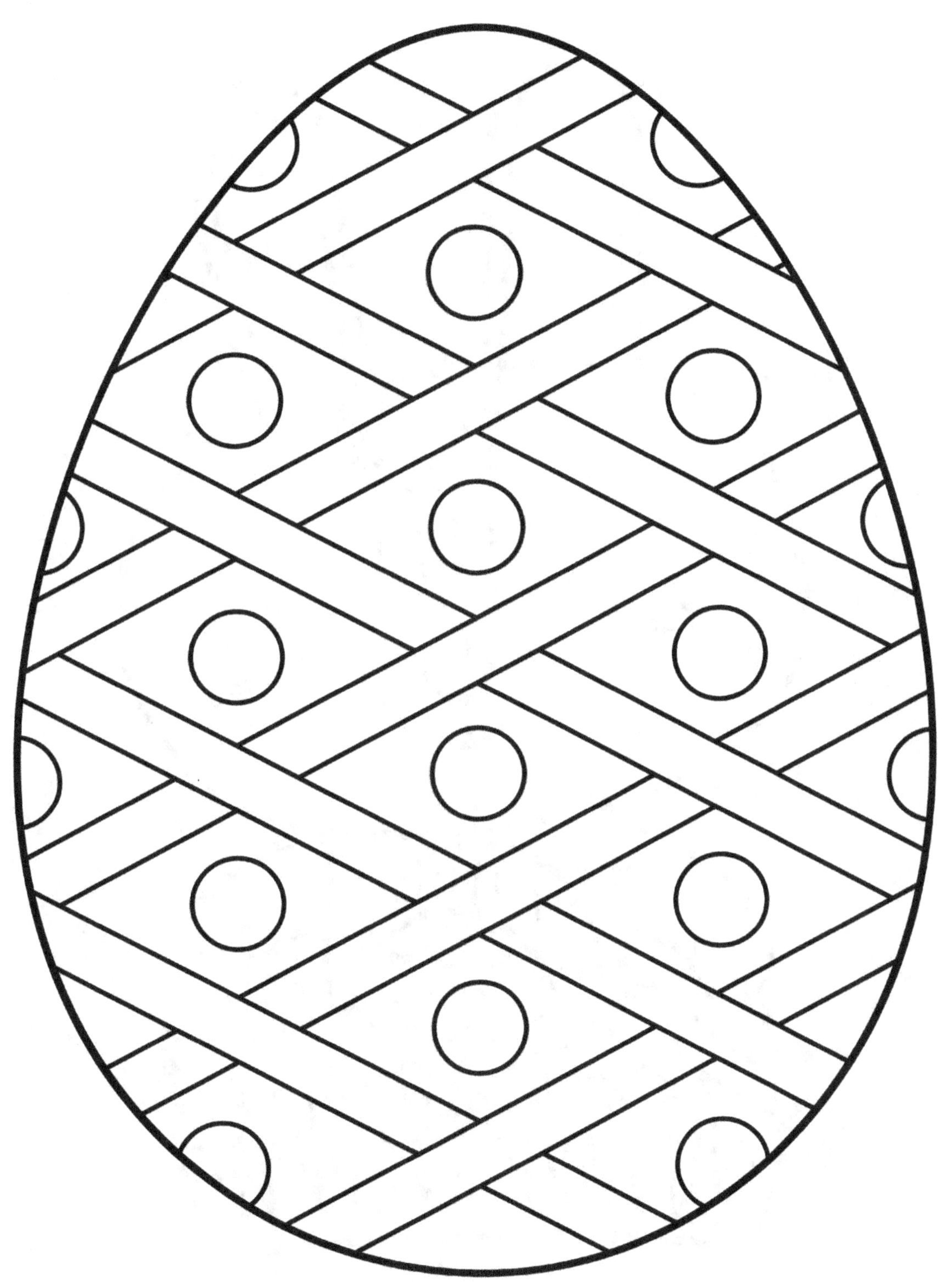

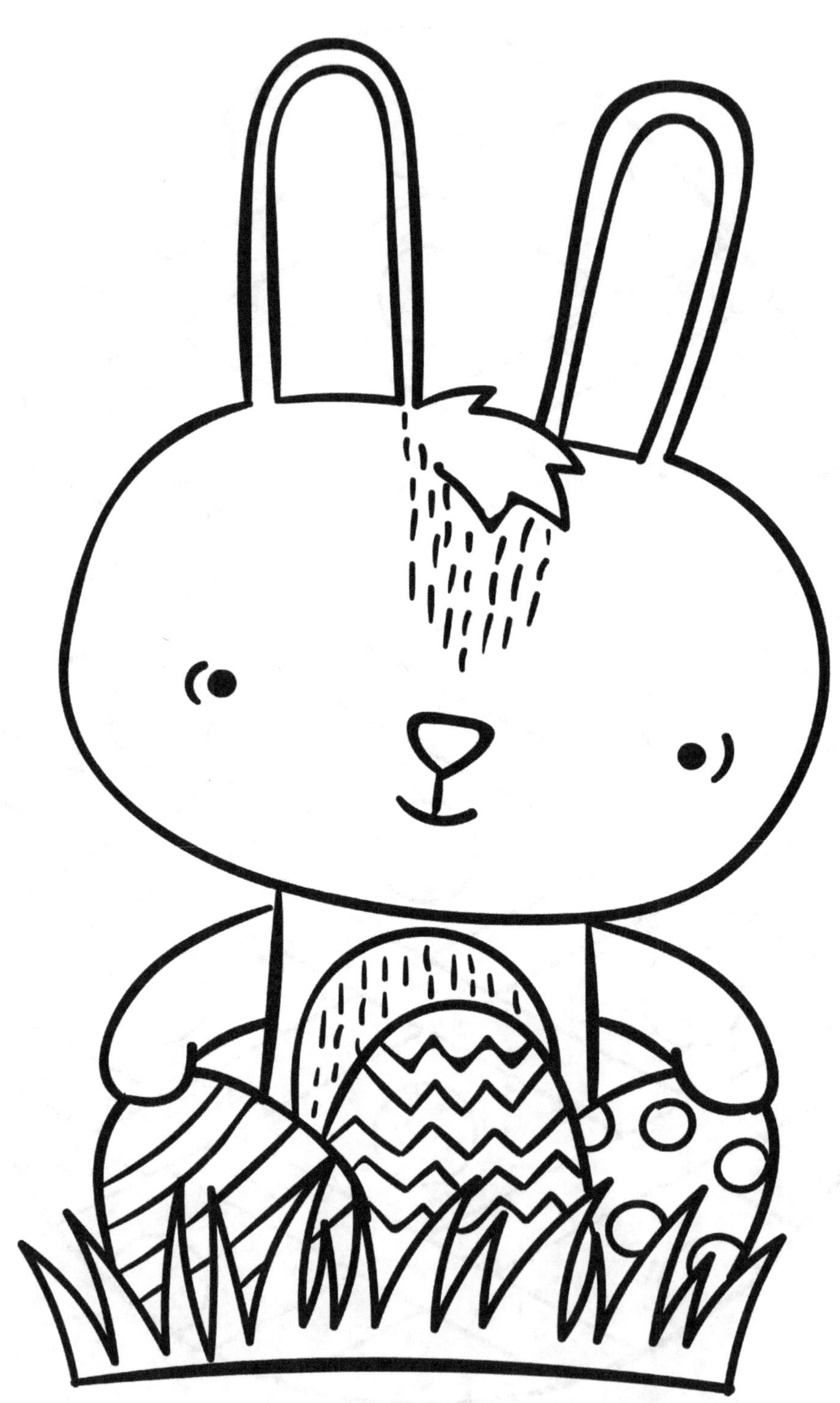

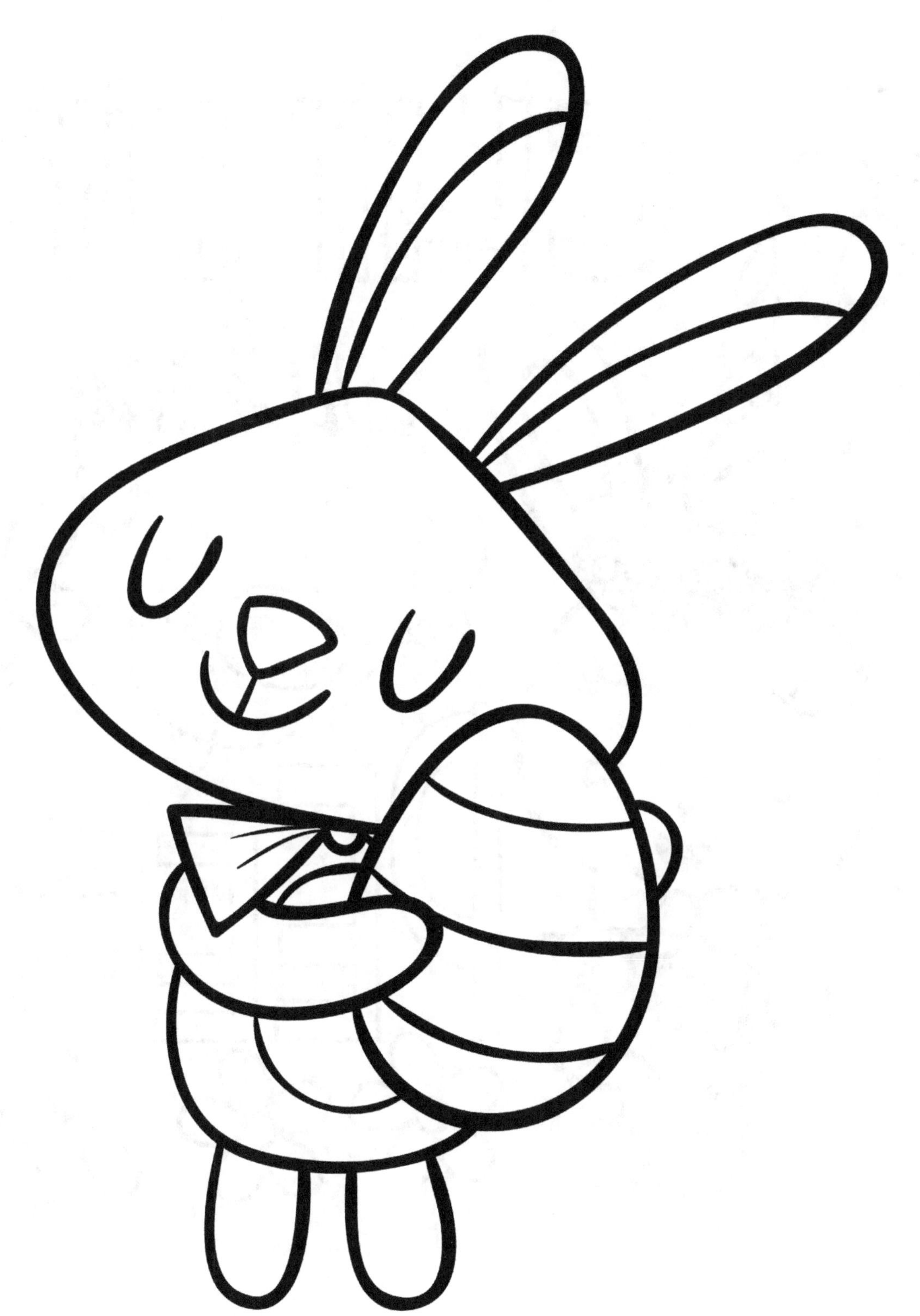

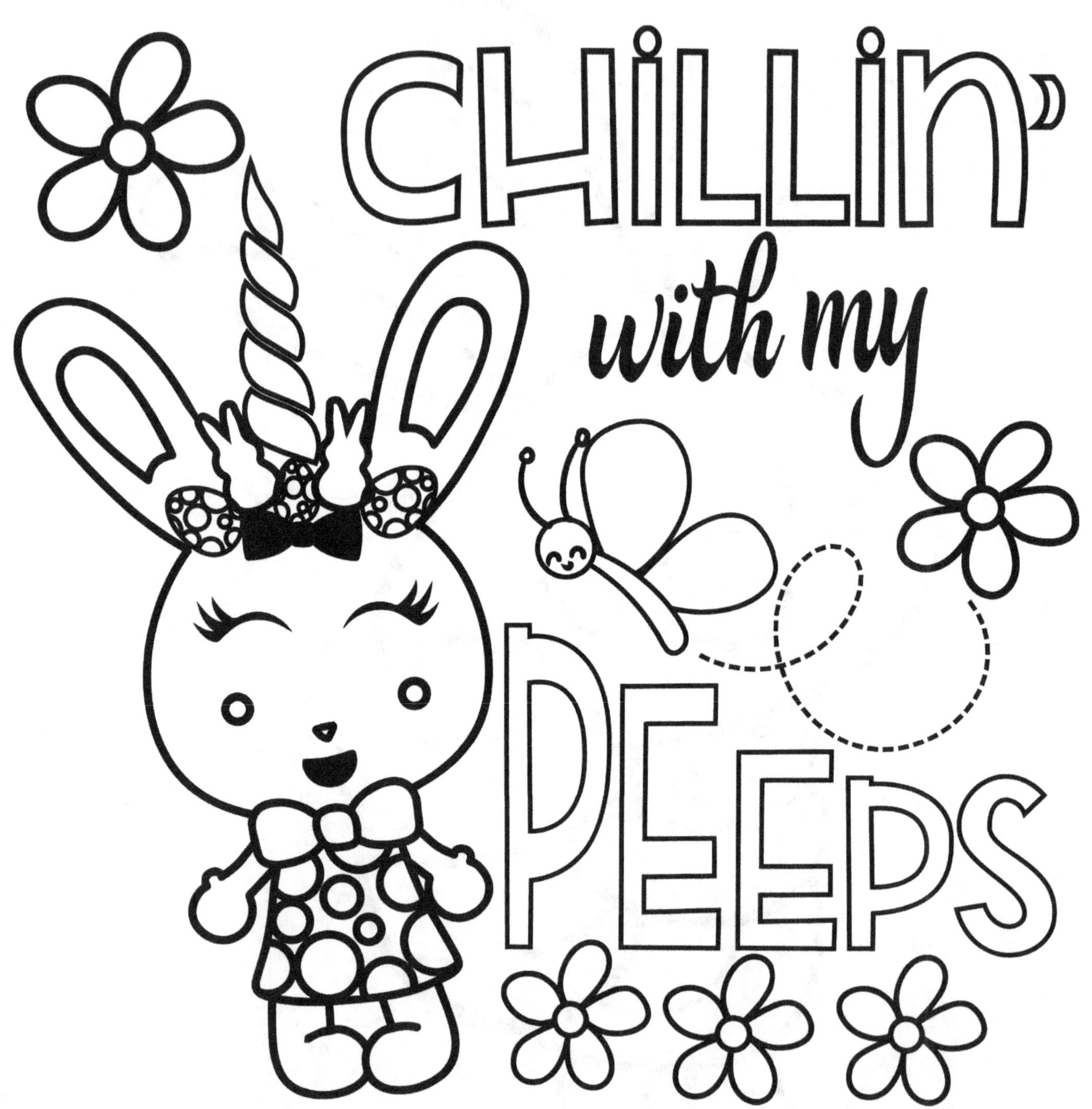

CHILLIN'
with my
PEEPS

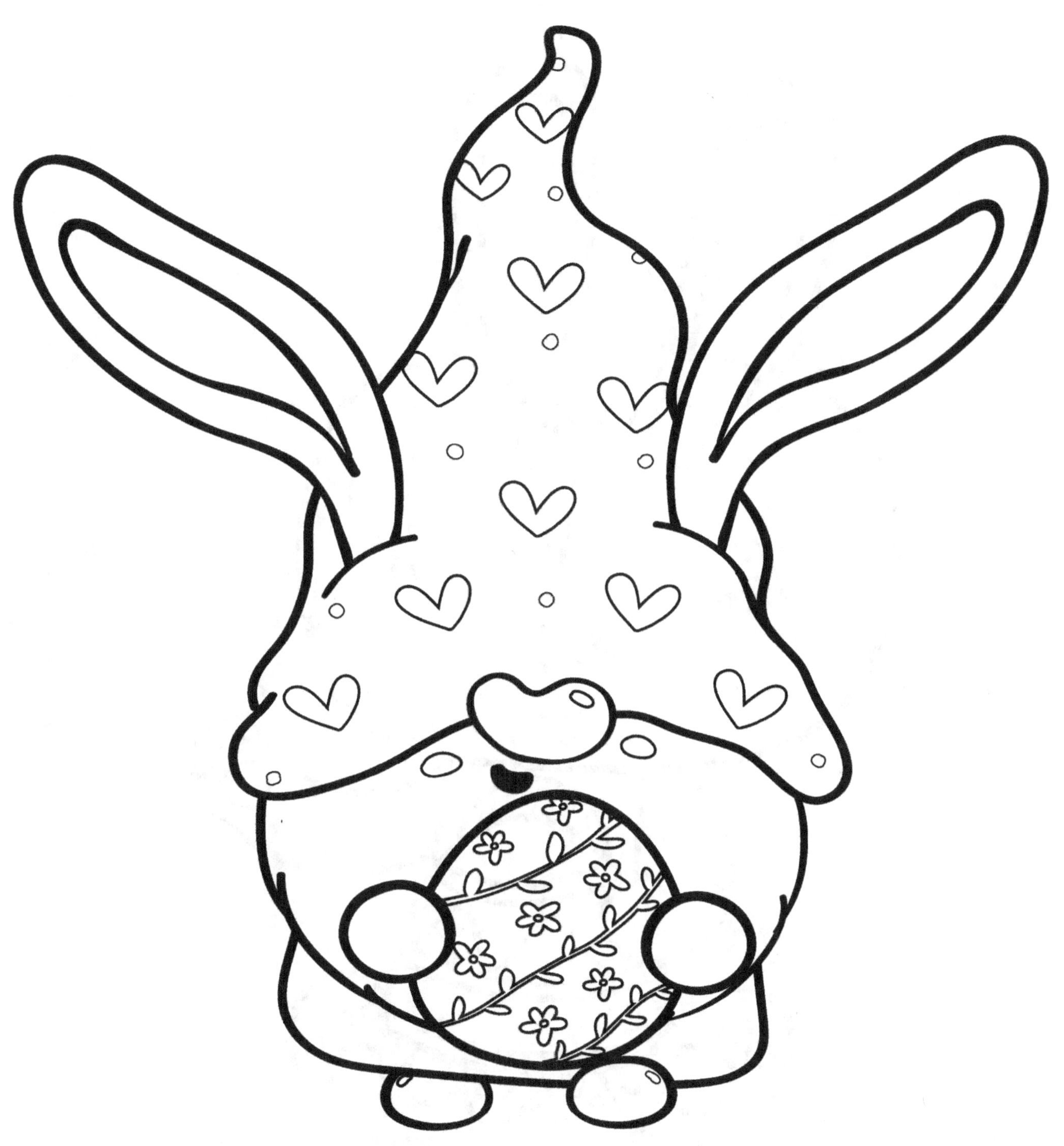

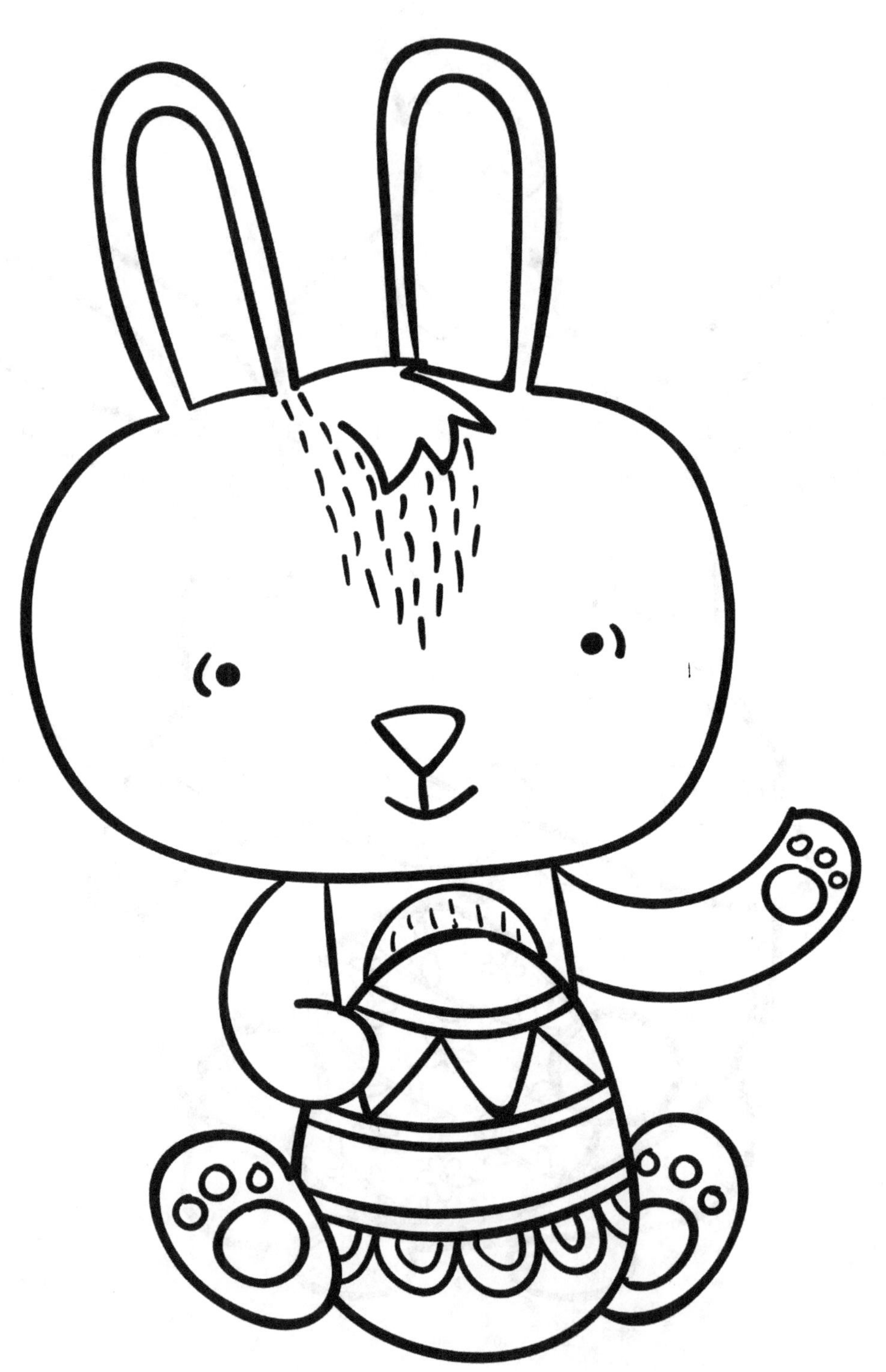

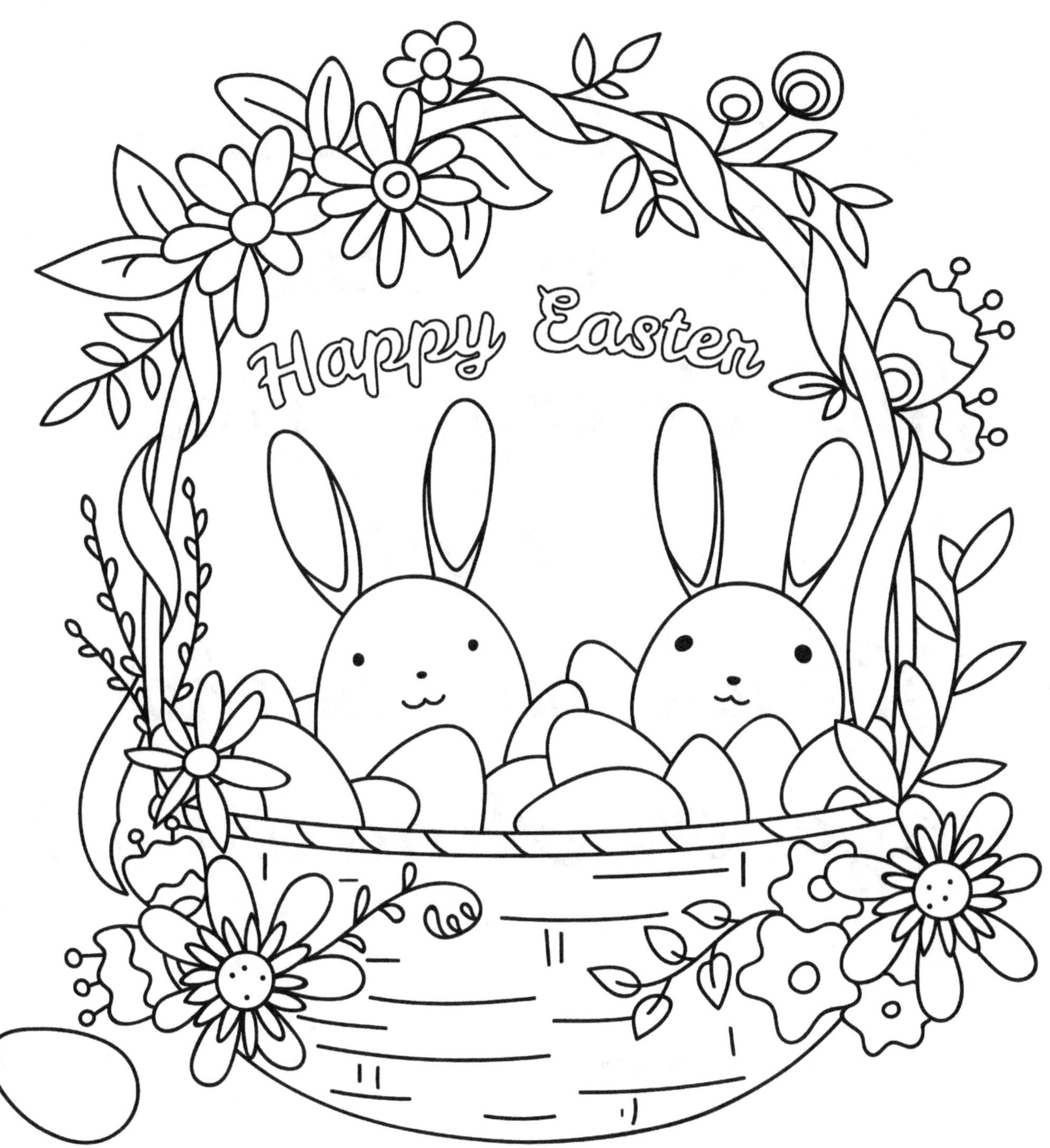
Happy Easter

Be on the lookout
for our other
Big Coloring Book
Titles!
Check our author
page on Amazon at:

https://www.amazon.com/Journals-ForYou/e/B08SDWYPJ3

www.ingramcontent.com/pod-product-compliance
Lightning Source LLC
Chambersburg PA
CBHW081251250726
48654CB00012B/1568